Anonymous

The morality of the East:

Extracted from the Koran of Mohammed: digested under alphabetical heads; with an introduction, and occasional remarks

Anonymous

The morality of the East:
Extracted from the Koran of Mohammed: digested under alphabetical heads; with an introduction, and occasional remarks

ISBN/EAN: 9783337729875

Printed in Europe, USA, Canada, Australia, Japan

Cover: Foto ©ninafisch / pixelio.de

More available books at **www.hansebooks.com**

THE MORALITY OF THE EAST;

EXTRACTED FROM THE

KORAN of MOHAMMED:

DIGESTED UNDER ALPHABETICAL HEADS,

WITH AN INTRODUCTION, AND OCCASIONAL REMARKS.

Unto every of you have we given a law, and an open path; and, if God had pleafed, he had furely made you one people; but he hath thought fit to give you different laws, that he might try you in that which he hath given you refpectively. Therefore ftrive to excel each other in good works; unto God fhall ye all return, and then will he declare unto you that concerning which ye have difagreed. KORAN, *chap.* v.

LONDON:
Printed for W. N ı c o ı ı, in St. Paul's Church-Yard. MDCCLXVI.

[Price Two Shillings, fewed.]

INTRODUCTION.

IN order to form a proper judgment of men and things, it will be incumbent on us to generalize our ideas, to extend them beyond the contemplation of our own countrymen, the profeſſors of the ſame religious principles, and beyond local modes of thinking: to mankind collectively, and ſubjects abſtractedly; overlooking the ſeveral denominations by which humankind are broken into independent communities, and ſeparate brotherhoods; whether by the barriers of nature, the policy of governments, or meer obſtinate tenacity of particular opinions.

It is very natural for thoſe who exerciſe dominion over mankind, whether in a civil or religious capacity, to purſue all ſuch meaſures as may tend to confirm and extend their authority over their subjects; and nothing contributes more to these purposes, than a careful inculcation of such intellectual or local prejudices, as may perpetuate exclusive distinctions, confirm parties in their tenets of separation, and by teaching them directly or indirectly to detest each other, attach them the more closely under their respective leaders. However knowledge may be reproached with *puffing* men up, it is ignorance that puffeth up zeal.

A persuasion in favour of particular systems of belief, has often no more foundation than an internal evidence, and arguments which carry no conviction with them beyond a ridge of mountains, or a cross a river: moreover the common pleas urged in favour of one, will frequently admit of being adapted with equal advantage to the support of any other. Nor has there been want of martyrs who have laid down their lives in testimony of their sincerity for all opinions, even the most contradictory: a
native

native of Rome, Paris, or London, might by an education at Constantinople, have become a strenuous assertor of the mission of Mohammed; or by receiving his ideas at Pekin, have rejected all other legislators and prophets, in favour of Fohi and Confucius.

The coincidence of truth with utility, and the reciprocal proof they afford of each other, have been strongly insisted on by the learned Bishop of Gloucester, in his Divine Legation of Moses. It follows, that such truths which have no test of utility to which they may be brought, can be but of small importance to mankind. Yet of this nature have been most of those points, the establishing or rooting out of which, have spread so much horror and desolation in various parts of the earth. This in great measure arose from a persuasion of the universality of truth; and a fond notion that the true religion ought to be the only religion: hence every one has strove, by all imaginable practices, both fair and foul, (the end

INTRODUCTION.

sanctifying the means,) to be that universal church. But, if their several dogmas were to be estimated by their means of propagation, on the good Bishop's plan of utility to mankind;—the probable result is left to the reader's conception.

An elegant writer has argued this point of the required universality as the evidence of a true religion, in a very ingenious manner, as follows.—' On what incomprehen-
' sible plan, must the wise Disposer of all things
' proceed, to suffer men thus to bewilder
' themselves in the labyrinths of error, and
' from thence to plunge into the gulphs of
' wickedness and misery, when the least direc-
' tion from his omnipotent hand, would lead
' them through the flowery paths of truth,
' to virtue and felicity? Strange! that he
' has not given them reason sufficient to
' perform this important office! Stranger!
' that if ever he condescended to assist that
' reason with his infinite wisdom, even the
' religion that results from that supernatural
assistance,

INTRODUCTION.

' affiftance, fhould ftill be deficient in almoft
' every one of the principal requifites necef-
' fary toward accomplifhing the great and
' beneficent ends it was defigned for! that
' it fhould want univerfality to render it im-
' partial, authenticity to make it demonftra-
' ble, perfpicuity to make it intelligible, and
' policy to make it ufeful to mankind: that
' it fhould immediately have been corrupt-
' ed, and from that corruption been pro-
' ductive of all the mifery and wickednefs it
' feemed calculated to prevent. But on exa-
' mination we fhall find, that thefe evils, like
' all thofe of which we have before treated,
' owe their exiftence to no defect of good-
' nefs or power in God, but to the imper-
' fection of man, and their own neceffity:
' that is, to the impracticability of giving a
' perfect religion to an imperfect creature.'*

Whether this folution of the difficulty
will be fatisfactory to philofophers and pole-

---

* Origin of Evil. Letter VI.

mics, must be left to philosophers and polemics to determine.

Human nature is nearly the same in all places and at all times; it is the education bestowed on it, that stamps the varieties between the antient and modern; and together with an allowance for the influence of climate, between the European and the Asiatic. Legislative policy working upon national pride, has given rise to many particular missions, and exclusive claims to the favour of Heaven; which have been supported by various means as circumstances have dictated. But on whatever wild reveries they may have been founded, or however common sense may be insulted by their rites and ceremonies; the relative duties of humanity have not so often been mistaken, at least within the circle of the votaries of the same persuasion. These being of general concern, and having their foundation, not in the fancy, but in our feelings; mankind were not so likely to be led astray by

the

INTRODUCTION. 7

the intoxications of heated imaginations with regard to them; especially when we reflect that no community can subsist under a disregard of matters of such immediate importance.

To form an impartial estimate of the intrinsic merits of any religion, it may be necessary to pass over all the supernaturals wherewith it is embellished, and recommended to the veneration of its votaries; and to examine the tendency of those practical duties enjoined for the conduct of man toward man: this is the infallible test, the golden rule, laid down by our Messiah, and brought home to the apprehensions of those to whom it is addressed, by a familiar and most happy allusion. We are not only invited to judge for ourselves what is right;* but are referred to a fruit tree as a guide to our judgment: *Do men gather grapes of thorns, or figs of thistles? Even so every good*

* Luke xii. 57.

tree bringeth forth good fruit: but a corrupt tree bringeth forth evil fruit,—Wherefore, by their fruits ye shall know them.*

It is hoped this publication may not be misconstrued, or misrepresented, into a design to recommend Mohammedism to Christians; or in any measure to set the Koran in competition with the Holy Scriptures: God be thanked *we* are not reduced to derive our morals from any such source; as, (notwithstanding the representations of the ingenious gentleman just quoted) drinking the waters of life from a purer stream. The only view was, by undergoing a piece of drudgery, to present the public with what may at least be esteemed a curiosity by numbers who might be disgusted with the toil of acquiring it, viz. from a heap of jargon to extract and throw into a concise view, the moral maxims of an Arab, whose dictates have been received by such extensive regions, in the fairest and most delightful

* Matt. vii. 16, 17, 20.

INTRODUCTION.

quarter of the globe. May one farther motive be tolerated? The operations of that zeal, which is not according to knowledge, are so violent in some, contract the operations of the mind into so narrow a circle, and warp the judgment so far from the truth; that we ought to pray for that degree of Laodicean lukewarmness, which may preserve to us the free and perfect use of our rational faculties: and there are many sincere and well meaning people, to whom it may be some information, to find that mussulmen, although painted with such fierce whiskers on sign posts at inn doors, are taught by their law, understand, and practice, the moral duties; to a degree that may shame many who profess a better religion: this compilation may therefore not be without its use in extending that charity of opinion toward our fellow creatures, which is so little understood, though it constitutes so fundamental an article of the christian religion.—*And now abideth faith, hope,*

hope, charity, these three; but the greatest of these is charity.*

In faith and hope, the world may disagree;
But all mankind's concern is *charity*. POPE.

Mohammed arose at a most convenient time for a man of talents to give birth to a new reform of religion. Born in the midst of pagan darkness, and monkish barbarism, religion was debased to such a degree, as rendered the dictates of that subtil Arab really sublime, when compared with the grossness of pagan idolatry on the one hand, and with the then mixture of christian idolatry and jargon on the other. Perhaps a more concise clear and just account of Mohammed may not easily be found or collected, than is contained in the learned Mosheim's Ecclesiastical History; with which we will therefore enrich our little compendium of his morals.

'A new and most powerful enemy to the
'Christian cause started up in Arabia A. D.
'612,

---

* 1 Cor. xiii. 13.

INTRODUCTION.

‘ 612, under the reign of Heraclius. This
‘ was Mahomet, an illiterate man,* but en-
‘ dowed by nature with the moſt flowing
‘ and attractive eloquence, and with a vaſt
‘ and penetrating genius,† diſtinguiſhed alſo
‘ by

* ‘Mahomet himſelf exprefly declared, that he
‘ was totally ignorant of all branches of learn-
‘ ing and ſcience, and was even unable either to
‘ write or read: and his followers have drawn
‘ from this ignorance an argument in favour of
‘ the divinity of his miſſion, and of the religion
‘ he taught. It is, however, ſcarcely credible,
‘ that his ignorance was ſuch as it is here de-
‘ ſcribed, and ſeveral of his ſect have called in
‘ queſtion the declarations of their chief relat-
‘ ing to this point. See Chardin, *Voyages en*
‘ *Perſe*, tom. iv. p. 33, 34. If we conſider that
‘ Mahomet carried on, for a conſiderable time,
‘ a ſucceſsful commerce in Arabia, and the ad-
‘ jacent countries, this alone will convince us,
‘ that he muſt have been, in ſome meaſure, in-
‘ ſtructed in the arts of reading, writing, and
‘ arithmetic, with the knowledge of which a
‘ merchant cannot diſpenſe.’

† ‘ The writers, to whom we are indebted for
‘ accounts of the life and religion of Mahomet,
‘ are enumerated by Fabricius, in his *Delectus et*
‘ *Syllabus*

' by the advantages he enjoyed from the
' place of his birth, which added a luftre
' to his name and his undertakings. This
' adventurous impoftor declared publickly,
' that he was commiffioned, by God, to de-
' ftroy polytheifm and idolatry, and then to
' reform, firft the religion of the Arabians,
' and afterwards the Jewifh and Chriftian
' worfhip. For thefe purpofes he delivered
' a new law, which is known by the name
' of the Koran,* or Alcoran; and having
' gained

' *Syllabus argumentor. p o re i a e relig. Chrifti-*
' *anæ*, cap. I. p. 733. To which we may add,
' Boulainvilliers, *Vie de Mahomet*, publifhed at
' London, in 8vo, in the year 1730, and which
' deferves rather the character of a romance, than
' of a hiftory. Gagnier, *Vie de Mahomet*, print-
' ed at Amfterdam, in two volumes in 8vo, in
' 1732, and commendable both for the learning
' and candour with which it appears to have been
' compofed; and, above all, the moft learned
' and judicious Sale's *Preliminary Difcourfe*, pre-
' fixed to his *English tranflation of the Koran*, § 2.

* ' For an account of the Koran, fee princi-
' pally the learned Sale's Preface to his English

INTRODUCTION.

'gained several victories over his enemies,
'he compelled an incredible multitude of
'persons, both in Arabia and the neighbour-
'ing nations, to receive his doctrine, and
'range themselves under his standards.
'Elated with this rapid and unexpected suc-
'cess, he extended yet further his ambitious
'views, and formed the vast and arduous
'project of founding an empire. Here
'again, success crowned his adventurous
'efforts; and his plan was executed with
'such intrepidity and impudence, that he
'died master of all Arabia, beside several
'adjacent provinces.

'It is, perhaps, impossible at this time, to
'form such an accurate judgment of the cha-
'racter, views, and conduct of Mahomet,
'as wou'd entirely satisfy the curiosity of a

'translation of that work. See also Vertot's *Dif-*
'*cours sur l' Alcoran*, which is subjoined to the
'third volume of his *History of the Knights of*
'*Malta*, and Chardin's *Voyages en Perse*, tom.
'ii. p. 251.'

'sagacious

'sagacious inquirer after truth. To give
' entire credit to the Grecian writers in this
' matter, is neither prudent nor safe, since
' their bitter resentment against this hostile in-
' vader led them to invent, without scruple or
' hesitation, fables and calumnies to blacken
' his character. The Arabians, on the other
' hand, are as little to be trusted to; as their
' historians are destitute of veracity and can-
' dour, conceal the vices and enormities of
' their chief, and represent him as the most
' divine person that ever appeared upon earth,
' and as the best gift of God to the world.
' Add to this, that a considerable part of Ma-
' homet's life, and indeed that part of it that
' would be the most proper to lead us to a true
' knowledge of his character, and of the
' motives from which he acted, is absolutely
' unknown. It is highly probable, that he
' was so deeply affected with the odious and
' abominable superstition which dishonoured
' his country, that it threw him into a cer-
' tain fanatical disorder of mind, and made
' him

' him really imagine that he was superna-
' turally commissioned to reform the religion
' of the Arabians, and to restore among them
' the worship of one God. It is, however,
' at the same time undoubtedly evident, that,
' when he saw his enterprize crowned with
' the desired success, he made use of impi-
' ous frauds to establish the work he had so
' happily begun, deluded the giddy and cre-
' dulous multitude by various artifices, and
' even forged celestial visions to confirm his
' authority and remove the difficulties that
' frequently arose in the course of his af-
' fairs. This mixture of imposture is, by
' no means, incompatible with a spirit of
' enthusiasm; for the fanatic, through the un-
' guided warmth of zeal, looks often upon
' the artifices, that are useful to his cause,
' as pious and acceptable to the supreme
' being, and therefore deceives when he can
' do it with impunity.* The religion which
                                    ' Mahomet

'Mahomet taught is certainly different from
what it would have been, if he had met
with no oppofition, in the propagation of
his opinions. The difficulties he had to
encounter obliged him to yield, in fome
refpects, to the reigning fyftems; the ob-
ftinate attachment of the Arabians to the
religion of their anceftors on the one hand,
and the fond hope of gaining over to
his caufe both the Jews and Chriftians or
the other, engaged, no doubt, this fanatical impoftor to admit into his fyftem feveral tenets, which he would have rejected
without hefitation, had he been free from
the reftraints of ambition and artifice.

* 'This, methinks, is the beft way of ad-
jufting the controverfy that has been carried on
by fome learned men upon this curious queftion,
viz. Whether Mahomet was a fanatic, or an
impoftor. See Bayle's *Dictionary*, at the article
Mahomet. Ockleys's *Conqueft of Syria, Perfia, and Egypt by the Saracens*, Vol. I. p. 62.
Sale's Preface to his tranflation of the *Alcoran*, § 2.

'The

INTRODUCTION. 17

'The rapid fuccefs, which attended the
'propagation of this new religion, was ow-
'ing to caufes that are plain and evident,
'and muft remove, or rather prevent, our
'furprize, when they are attentively confi-
'dered. The terror of Mahomet's arms,
'and the repeated victories which were gain-
'ed by him and his fucceffors, were, no
'doubt, the irrefiftible argument that per-
'fuaded fuch multitudes to embrace his re-
'ligion, and fubmit to his dominion. Be-
'fides, his law was artfully and marvelloufly
'adapted to the corrupt nature of man;
'and, in a more particular manner, to the
'manners and opinions of the eaftern na-
'tions, and the vices to which they were
'naturally addicted; for the articles of faith
'which it propofed were few in number,
'and extremely fimple; and the duties it re-
'quired were neither many, nor difficult,
'nor fuch as were incompatible with the em-
'pire of appetites and paffions *. It is to be

* 'See Reland, *De religione Mahumedica.*
'Sale's *Preliminary Difcourfe.*'

C 'obferved

'observed further, that the gross ignorance,
'under which the Arabians, Syrians, Persians,
'and the greatest part of the eastern nations,
'laboured at this time, rendered many an
'easy prey to the artifice and eloquence of
'this bold adventurer. To these causes of
'the progress of Mahometism, we may add the
'bitter dissentions and cruel animosities that
'reigned among the Christian sects, particular-
'ly the Greeks, Nestorians, Eutychians, and
'Monophysites, dissentions that filled a great
'part of the east with carnage, assassina-
'tions, and such detestable enormities, as
'rendered the very name of Christianity odi-
'ous to many. We might add here, that the
'Monophysites and Nestorians, full of re-
'sentment against the Greeks, from whom
'they had suffered the bitterest and most in-
'jurious treatment, assisted the Arabians in
'the conquest of several provinces *, into

* 'See Ockley's *Conquest of Syria Persia, and
'Egypt by the Saracens*, the first part of which was
'published at *London*, in the year 1708, and the
'second in 1717.'

'which,

' which, of consequence, the religion of
' Mahomet was afterwards introduced.
' Other causes of the sudden progress of that
' religion, will naturally occur to such as
' consider attentively its spirit and genius,
' and the state of the world at this time.

' After the death of Mahomet, which
' happened A. D. 632, his followers, led on
' by an amazing intrepidity, and a fanati-
' cal fury, and assisted, as we have already
' observed, by those Christians whom the
' Greeks had treated with such severity, ex-
' tended their conquests beyond the limits of
' Arabia, and subdued Syria, Persia, Egypt,
' and other countries under their dominion.
' On the other hand, the Greeks exhausted
' with civil discords, and wholly occupied
' by intestine troubles, were unable to stop
' these intrepid conquerors in their rapid
' career.

' For some time these enthusiastic invaders
' used their prosperity with moderation, and
' treated the Christians, and particularly
' those

'those among them who rejected the decrees
'of the councils of Ephesus and Chalcedon,
'with the utmost indulgence and lenity.
'But as an uninterrupted course of success
'and prosperity, renders too generally cor-
'rupt mortals insolent and imperious, so
'the moderation of this victorious sect de-
'generated by degrees, into severity; and
'they treated the Christians, at length, ra-
'ther like slaves, than citizens, loading them
'with unsupportable taxes, and obliging
'them to submit to a variety of vexations
'and oppressive measures.

'The progress, however, of this trium-
'phant sect received a considerable check by
'the civil dissensions which arose among
'them immediately after the death of Ma-
'homet. Abubeker and Ali, the former
'the father-in law, and the latter the son-
'in-law, of this pretended prophet, aspired
'both to succeed him in the empire which
'he had erected. Upon this arose a tedious
'and cruel contest, whose flame reached to

'succeed-

'succeeding ages, and produced that schism
'which divided the Mahometans into two
'great factions, whose separation not only
'gave rise to a variety of opinions and rites,
'but also excited the implacable hatred, and
'the most deadly animosities. Of these
'factions, the one acknowledged Abubeker
'as the true *calif*, or successor of Mahomet,
'and its members were distinguished by the
'name of Sonnites; while the other adher-
'ed to Ali, and were known by the title
'of Schiites*. Both however adhered to the
'Alcoran as a divine law, and the rule of
'faith and manners; to which, indeed, the
'former added, by way of interpretation,
'the *sonna*, i. e. a certain law which they
'looked upon as descended from Mahomet
'by oral tradition, and which the Schiites
'refused to admit. Among the Sonnites,
'or followers of Abubeker, we are to

* See Reland, *De religione Turcica*, lib. i. p. 36. 70. 74. 85. Chardin's *Voyage en Perse*, tom. ii. p. 236.

'reckon

'reckon the Turks, Tartars, Arabians, Africans, and the greatest part of the Indian Mahometans; whereas the Persians, and the subjects of the Grand Mogul are generally considered as the followers of Ali; though the latter indeed seem rather to observe a strict neutrality in this contest.

'Besides these two grand factions, there are other subordinate sects among the Mahometans, which dispute with warmth concerning several points of religion, though without violating the rules of mutual toleration *. Of these sects there are four, which far surpass the rest in point of reputation and importance †.'

When we consider the malignant zeal which so frequently poisons the pens engaged in church-history and controversy, the

---

* 'For an account of the Mahometan sects, see
'Hottinger. *Histor. Orient.* lib. ii. cap. vi. p.
'340. Ricaut, *Etat. de l'Empire Ottoman*, livr.
'ii. p. 242. Chardin's *Voyages en Perse*, tom. ii.
'p. 236. Sale's *Preliminary Discourse*, § 8.'
† Mosheim's *Eccles. Hist.* vol. i. p. 313.

candid

candid manner of this gentleman, calls for a remark. To this account of Mohammed, we will add from the testimony of Mr. Sale, the Mohammedan notion of the Deity; which some perhaps may be heterodox enough to think most unexceptionable in that very article on which an exception to it is founded.

'That both Mohammed, and those among his followers, who are reckoned orthodox, had, and continue to have, just and true notions of God and his attributes, (always excepting their obstinate and impious rejecting of the Trinity) appears so plain from the Koran itself, and all the Mohammedan divines, that it would be loss of time to refute those who suppose the God of Mohammed to be different from the true God *.'——

To the same import also is the following passage from a respectable French writer, to

* Prelim. Discourse, § 4. p. 93.

whose other learning was joined a personal knowledge of the Ottomans.

'Of all false religions, the Mahometan is
'the most dangerous, because it not only
'strongly flatters the senses, but in many
'points also agrees with Christianity. Ma-
'hometism is founded on the knowledge of
'the true God, the Creator of all things,
'upon the love of our neighbour, the purifi-
'cation of the body, and a quiet peaceable
'life. It abhors idols, and the worship of
'them is strictly prohibited *.'

Indeed Mohammed appears to have been a zealous asserter of the unity of Deity; taking frequent occasion throughout the Koran to insist on it as the fundamental point of religion, and to denounce severe vengeance against those who associate other names or relations with God. If it may be pardonable to indulge a little in conjecture, it may not appear perhaps the most absurd

---

* Tournefort's Voyages, English edition, vol. II. p. 282.

that

INTRODUCTION. 25

that has been hazarded, when we reflect how extensive the spread of Mohammedism has been, if we attribute somewhat of that reformation from Romish idolatry, the seeds of which continued taking root, long before they were cultivated for political purposes; to the indirect influence of the doctrine of the unity of the great God of the universe, who is truly, if, in an erroneous manner, the pure object of eastern adoration. That this conjecture may not be laughed out of countenance, without something farther being urged to apologise for making it; the reader is requested to consider, that while the Christian world were daily worshipping and eating their God in the form and substance of a cake; while they were debasing and wasting their rational powers on scholastic subtilties, founded in absurdity; the Asiatics adored a God whom they were taught to conceive in these terms—' God! there is no God but he; the
' living, the self-subsisting; neither slumber
' nor sleep seizeth him; to him belongeth
' what-

'whatsoever is in heaven, and on earth. Who
'he is that can intercede with him, but
'through his good pleasure? He knoweth
'that which is past, and that which is to
'come to them, and they shall not compre-
'hend any thing of his knowledge, but so
'far as he pleaseth. His throne is extended
'over heaven and earth, and the preserva-
'tion of both is no burthen unto him. He
'is the high, the mighty *.' These are ex-
pressions which must strike with their sublimity, even those who despise the Arabian
apostle that dictated them.

Were it necessary to enter into a compa-
rison between the Mohammedan system and
popery, a thinking man would not hesitate
long in deciding to which the preference was
due: for to instance only in another particular; whereas the penances and atone-
ments for sins in the latter, are chiefly directed to useless rituals, and unprofitable

* Koran, chap. ii. vol. I. p. 47.

mortifications; the expiations of the former have generally a benevolent direction to the good of society; as to the freeing the captive, to feeding and cloathing the hungry, &c. See some instances of this kind, under the articles MURDER, OATHS, &c. beside other instances which do not come so directly under our view.

That the more northern nations have improved so happily this first principle of theology, which dawned on them through the Mohammedan system; and perhaps assisted them in recovering and refining the Christian religion from the rubbish under which it was overwhelmed by craft and ignorance, may be partly accounted for from those principles which will equally explain why they have asserted and maintain, the natural and civil rights of mankind, in a greater or less degree, while the soft nations of the east, continue from century to century the dispirited subjects to an absolute and fixed despotism. Much

Much having been said relating to the sensuality of Mohammed's paradise, it may not be disagreeable to the reader to see from the Koran one of the best connected descriptions of it.

'When the inevitable day of judgment
'shall suddenly come, no soul shall charge
'the prediction of its coming with false-
'hood: it will abase some, and exalt others.
'When the earth shall be shaken with a
'violent shock; and the mountains shall be
'dashed in pieces, and shall become as dust
'scattered abroad; and ye shall be separated
'into three distinct classes: the companions
'of the right hand, (how happy shall the
'companions of the right hand be!) and the
'companions of the left hand; (how miser-
'able shall the companions of the left hand
'be!) and those who have preceded others
'in the faith, shall precede them to para-
'dise. These are they who shall approach
'near unto God: they shall dwell in gar-
'dens of delight: (there shall be many of the
'former

INTRODUCTION.

'former religions, and few of the laſt.)
'Repoſing on couches adorned with gold
'and precious ſtones; ſitting oppoſite to one
'another thereon. Youths which ſhall con-
'tinue in their bloom for ever, ſhall go
'round about to attend them, with goblets
'and beakers, and a cup of flowing wine:
'their heads ſhall not ake by drinking the
'ſame, neither ſhall their reaſon be diſturb-
'ed: and with fruits of the ſorts which they
'ſhall chuſe, and the fleſh of birds of the
'kind which they ſhall deſire. And there
'ſhall accompany them fair damſels, having
'large black eyes, reſembling pearls hidden
'in their ſhells, as a reward for that which
'they ſhall have wrought. They ſhall not
'hear therein any vain diſcourſe, or any
'charge of ſin, but only the ſalutation,
'Peace! Peace! And the companions of
'the right hand, (how happy ſhall the com-
'panions of the right hand be!) ſhall have
'their abode among lote trees, free from
'thorns, and trees of mauz, loaded regularly
'with

'with their produce from top to bottom; under an extended shade, near a flowing water, and amidst fruits in abundance, which shall not fail, nor shall be forbidden to be gathered: and they shall repose themselves on lofty beds. Verily we have created the damsels of paradise by a peculiar creation: and we have made them virgins beloved by their husbands, of equal age with them; for the delight of the companions of the right hand *.'

The heaven declared in our Scripture is infinitely more refined and pure from carnal delights than this of the Koran; but for that very reason, not so well calculated to attract mankind in general. We are there told that in heaven none is either married, or given in marriage †. It is not directed to our feelings, but to our understandings, professedly abstracted from all worldly objects; and even from ourselves, as imperfect be-

* Koran, ch. 56. † Matt. xxii. 30.

ings; corruption being then to put on incorruption *. This it was that gave a certain theatrical genius, admirably suited to an acceptance of Mohammed's promises, the opportunity to pass his well known profane jest on it. The great publisher of our religion did not purpose to captivate the desires of men in their corrupt unregenerate state, and therefore gives them to understand, that as such they were not heirs of the promises; and that *strait is the gate, and narrow is the way, which leadeth unto life, and few there be that find it* †; for few men reason so well as to apprehend the excellence and sublimity of joys they do not feel.

Mohammed on the other hand, ensured the affections of his followers, by suiting his promises more to their feelings as men; and though the sanction of punishment is nearly alike in both, he has opened a broad way to their expectations, and many there be

* 1 Cor. xv. 42, &c. † Matt. vii. 14.

who

who travel therein. But let us in charity hope that it will not lead to destruction, those sincerely upright mussulmen, whose conduct may shew that they understand what they owe to their fellow creatures, though they may be milled in their apprehensions as to matters which even Christians do not in all respects agree concerning. Surely while we revere our Bible, we must believe there is some truth and meaning in passages which extend the mercy of God as far as the sun extends its rays, or the showers refresh the earth.

What doth the Lord require of thee, but to do justly, and to love mercy, and to walk humbly with thy God *. *Of a truth — God is no respecter of persons; but in every nation, he that feareth him, and worketh righteousness, is accepted with him* †.

Reflections on the obvious disparity every where observable, between precept and prac-

---

* Micah vi. 8.   † Acts x. 34, 35.

tice,

tice, are too trite to be infifted on now as new obfervations; nor will they appear peculiarly applicable on the prefent occafion. The Koran directs what true muffulmen ought to be; travellers will inform us what they are: and if we confult Mr. Tournefort, a perfon of known talents and unimpeached veracity, who travelled through great part of the Levant on botanical refearches, at the command of Louis XIV. we fhall be enabled to conceive fome idea of the prefent ftate of the government, religion, and private manners of the Turks, (who, though not the only muffulmen, are the moft diftinguifhed part of them) from actual obfervations, on which we may fafely rely.

The ottoman government is very well characterized by M. Tournefort in the following paffages; by which it will appear how neceffary it is in our prefent enquiry to diftinguifh between the government and the people.

'Thofe

'Those, who do not reflect on the original of this empire, discern at first sight, that the Turkish government is extremely severe, and almost tyrannical; but if we consider that it began in war, and that the first Ottomans were, from father to son, the most formidable conquerors of their age, we shall not be surprised, that they set no other limits to their power than merely their will.

'Could it be expected that princes, who owed their greatness solely to their arms, should divest themselves of their right of conquest, in favour of their slaves? It is natural for an empire which is founded in a time of peace, and the people of which make choice of a chief to govern them, to be mild and gentle, and the authority of it may, in a manner, be divided and shared; but the first Sultans owed their promotion purely to their own valour, and being full of maxims of war, affected to have a blind obedience, to punish with severity, and to keep their subjects under an inability to revolt; and in
' a word,

' a word, to be served only by persons who
' stood indebted to them for their fortune,
' whom they could advance without jealousy,
' and crush without injustice *.'

Thus much may suffice, as to the maxims on which this empire was first founded, and still subsists; the effects of it will not be difficult to conceive.

' Though the Turks, says M. Tourne-
' fort, imagine God gives prudence, and the
' other necessary talents, to those whom the
' Sultan raises to high employments; experi-
' ence often testifies the contrary. What
' capacity can pages have, who are trained up
' among eunuchs, who treat them with the
' bastinado for so long a time ? Would it not
' be better to promote youth by degrees, in
' an empire where no regard is had to birth ?
' Beside, these officers pass at a step, from a
' state of the utmost uneasiness and constraint,
' to such an extraordinary liberty, that it is

* Tournefort's Voyages, vol. ii. p. 228.

' impossible

'impossible they should not let loose their
' passions; and yet they are entrusted with
' the government of the most important pro-
' vinces. As they have neither abilities nor
' experience to perform the duties of their
' charge, they trust to their deputies, who are
' commonly great robbers, or spies of the
' grand Visier, to send him an account of
' their conduct. These new governors are
' forced also to pass through the hands of
' the Jews; for as they have nothing when
' they come from the Seraglio, they have re-
' course to those usurers, who lead them to
' all manner of rapine and extortion.—This
' evil would not be so extreme, if they would
' be content to receive it again by little and
' little; but as they are afraid every moment
' the Bassa should be strangled or removed,
' they never let a debt grow old, and the
' people must be squeezed to repay them*.'

Under such circumstances it is evident that nothing can be permanent at the Otto-

---

* Tournefort's Voyages, vol. ii. p. 242.

INTRODUCTION.

man Porte, and that it is a wheel inceſſantly turning *. Such is the government of a prince, whoſe ' empire extends from the
' Black Sea to the Red Sea; who has the bet-
' ter part of Africa; is maſter of all Greece,
' and even to the frontiers of Hungary and
' Poland; and who, in ſhort, can boaſt, that
' his predeceſſors or their grand Viſiers, have
' beſieged the capital of the weſtern empire,
' and have left only the gulph of Venice be-
' tween their dominions and Italy †.'

From the ſight of the wolves, let us now eaſe our akeing eyes, by contemplating the more placid manners of the ſheep; or, to drop the figure; from characters, which would make us deteſt human nature, let us, as is our intereſt, turn to the fairer ſide, and endeavour to reconcile ourſelves with it again: nor to do this, need we ſeek farther than amongſt the people of whom we are now treating. With regard to their religion, M. Tournefort agrees with what

* Tourn. Voy. p. 206.   † Id. p. 230,

we have already seen; and says —— 'The only article of faith the Mahometans have, is, that there is but one God, and that Mahomet is the messenger of God. As to the commandments, the Turks reduce them to five. I. To pray five times in a day. II. To fast in Lent, [or their month of Ramadan.] III. To give alms, and do works of charity. IV. To go in pilgrimage to Mecha. V. To suffer no filth upon their body. There are four other points added, but not as absolutely necessary to salvation. 1. To keep Friday a sabbath. 2. To be circumcised. 3. To drink no wine. 4. Not to eat swine's flesh, nor things strangled *. — They believe also that their prayers will not be heard, unless they first resolve firmly to forgive their enemies. It is for this reason that they never let a Friday pass without making a hearty reconciliation; and hence it is, that we never hear of any detraction or injury among the Turks †.'

* Tourn. Voy. p. 285. † Id. p. 296.

Where

Where their theological assumptions are so few and simple, and where, in consequence, such stress is laid on good works; there, if any where, we may expect to see the duties of humanity cultivated in an especial manner; and if the difference of religious sentiments will not permit us to respect them as brothers in Christ, we shall be obliged to allow them at least the character of being good Samaritans *.

We are told, that ' beside private alms,
' there is no nation which expends more upon
' public foundations than the Turks. Even
' they who have but a moderate fortune leave
' something after their death, to maintain a
' man to give water in the summer heats to
' drink to passengers, as they go along by the
' place where they are buried. Nor, (continues M. Tournefort) do I question but they
' would also have ordered vessels of wine,
' if Mahomet had not forbidden the use of

* Luke x. 30, &c.

' it.'

' it *.' — ' The sick visit the prisons, to dis-
' charge those who are arrested for debt:
' they are very careful to relieve persons who
' are bashfully ashamed of their poverty.
' How many families may one find, who
' have been ruined by fires, and are restored
' by charities! They need only present
' themselves at the doors of the mosques:
' they also go to their houses to comfort the
' afflicted. The diseased, and they who have
' the pestilence, are succoured by their neigh-
' bour's purse, and the parish funds. For the
' Turks, as Leunclavius observes set no
' bounds to their charities. They lay out
' money for repairing the high-ways, and
' making fountains for the benefit of passen-
' gers; and build hospitals, inns, baths,
' bridges, and mosques †.

' As charity and love of our neighbours
' are the most essential points of the Maho-
' metan religion, the high-ways are generally
' kept mighty well; and there are springs of

* Tourn. Voy. vol. ii. p. 304. † Id. p. 305.

' water

' water common enough, becaufe they are
' wanted for making the ablutions. The poor
' look after the conduit pipes, and thofe of
' tolerable fortune repair the caufeways. The
' neighbourhood joins together to build
' bridges over the deep roads, and contribute
' to the benefit of the public according to their
' power. The workmen take no hire, but
' find labourers and mafons gratis for the fe-
' veral forts of work. You may fee pitchers
' of water ftanding at the doors of the houfes
' in the towns, for the ufe of paffengers; and
' fome honeft muffulmen lodge themfelves un-
' der a fort of fheds, which they erect in the
' road, and do nothing elfe during the great
' heats, but get thofe who are weary to come
' in, and reft themfelves, and take a refrefh-
' ment.—The beggars themfelves, though
' there are very few to be feen, think they are
' obliged to give their fuperfluities to other
' poor folks; and carry their charity, or ra-
' ther vanity, to fuch an extreme, that they

' give

'give their leavings even to sufficient per-
'sons, who make no scruple to receive their
'bread, and to eat it, to shew how highly
'they esteem their virtue.

'The charity of the Mahometans is ex-
'tended also to animals and plants, and to
'the dead. They believe it is pleasing to
'God, since men who will use their reason
'want for nothing; whereas the animals,
'not having reason, their instinct often ex-
'poses them to seek their food with the loss
'of their lives. In considerable towns they
'sell victuals at the corners of the streets to
'give to the dogs; and some Turks, out of
'charity, have them cured of wounds, and
'especially of the mange, with which these
'creatures are miserably afflicted toward the
'end of their life; and we may see persons
'of good sense, out of mere devotion, carry
'straw to lay under the bitches which are
'going to whelp; and they build them small
'huts to shelter them and their puppies. We
'would

'would hardly believe there are endowments
'settled in form by will for maintaining a
'certain number of dogs and cats so many
'days in the week; yet this is commonly
'done; and there are people paid at Con-
'stantinople to see the donor's intention ex-
'ecuted, in feeding them in the streets. The
'butchers and bakers often set aside a small
'portion to bestow upon these animals: yet
'with all their charity, the Turks hate dogs,
'and never suffer them in their houses; and
'in a time of pestilence, they kill as many
'as they find, thinking these unclean crea-
'tures infect the air. On the contrary, they
'love cats very well, whether it be for their
'natural cleanliness, or because they sympa-
'thise with themselves in gravity; whereas
'dogs are wanton, sporting, and noisy.

'As to plants, the most devout among
'the Turks water them out of charity, and
'cultivate the earth where they grow, that
'they may thrive the better.——The good
'mussulmen believe they do in it a thing
'agreeable

'agreeable to God, who is the creator and
'preserver of all things *.'

Even though we should make a small matter of allowance for that exaggeration, which a gentleman might be betrayed into, who was surprized with so much benevolence and humanity, where perhaps he little expected to find them; enough will still remain; and the concurrent testimony of others, will all together sufficiently establish the fact, of the Turks being a most humane benevolent people. But to return.

The Koran, beside being composed at different times, dictated by, and suited to, different temporary occasions, exhibits much of that unconnected desultory manner, so observable in eastern compositions: so that far from having any discoverable relation among the divisions of it, or any seeming digest of the whole, it was often very difficult to select passages which admitted of be-

* Tournefort's Voyages, p. 308.

ing claffed under any diftinct head. Such as confifted of general precepts too mifcellaneous to belong with propriety to any one fubject, are placed together at the end, in their order of occurrence, under the title *General Precepts*; under which head the reader will find a number of promifcuous precepts and obfervations relating to moft of the fubjects fpecified under the foregoing divifions. Some paffages will appear dark and unaccountable to Europeans, from the want of a fufficient acquaintance with the eaftern ufages; and the collection might have been greatly fwelled by the admiffion of the notes of Arabian commentators, as given by Mr. Sale; but the fenfe of the text is as capable of being afcertained without their affiftance; there not appearing more agreement among them, than we experience among thofe who comment on a far fuperior compofition. It may be needlefs to add, that Mr. Sale's Verfion, the octavo edition of 1764, was

ufed

used on this occasion, as we possess no other English translation of any estimation.

As for the loose remarks added by the compiler under some particular passages, the writer presumes to say no more in their behalf, than that he gratified the present humour, in indulging those reflections and comparisons, which occurred on perusing the passages to which they relate; and hopes they may be pardoned, as they are detached and few. If they are rejected as impertinent or absurd, the writer must content himself with this consolation, that they are not the *only notes or commentaries*, which readers would have been willing to part with, to have had the text alone.

THE
MORALITY
OF THE
EAST.

THE MORALITY OF THE EAST.

ALMS.

OBSERVE the ſtated times of prayer, and pay your legal alms,* and bow down yourſelves with thoſe who bow down.

---

* What is to be underſtood by theſe legal alms which are thus referred to, is explained by the following paſſage in Sale's Preliminary Diſcourſe. 'Alms, according to the preſcriptions
' of the Mohammedan law, are to be given of
' five things; 1. Of cattle, that is to ſay, of ca-
' mels, kine, and ſheep. 2. Of money. 3. Of
' corn. 4. Of fruits, viz. dates and raiſins; and
' 5. of wares ſold. Of each of theſe a certain
' portion is to be given in alms, being uſually

down. Will ye command men to do juſtice, and forget your own ſouls? Yet ye read the book of the law; do ye not therefore underſtand? Chap. ii. Vol. i. p. 9.

Be

'one part in forty, or two and a half *per cent.*
'of the value. But no alms are due for them,
'unleſs they amount to a certain quantity or
'number; nor until a man has been in poſſeſ-
'ſion of them eleven months, he not being ob-
'liged to give alms thereout before the twelfth
'month is begun: nor are alms due for cattle
'employed in tilling the ground, or in carrying
'burdens. In ſome caſes, a much larger portion
'than the before mentioned, is reckoned due for
'alms: thus, of what is gotten out of mines, or
'the ſea, or by any art or profeſſion, over and
'above what is ſufficient for the reaſonable ſup-
'port of a man's family, and eſpecially where
'there is a mixture, or ſuſpicion, of unjuſt gain,
'a fifth part ought to be given in alms. More-
'over at the end of the faſt of Ramadan, every
'moſlem is obliged to give in alms for himſelf,
'and for every one of his family, if he has any,
'a meaſure of wheat, barley, dates, rice, or, other
'proviſions commonly eaten.'

'The legal alms were at firſt collected by Mo-
'hammed himſelf, who employed them as he
'thought fit, in the relief of his poor relations

'and

Be constant in prayer and give alms; and what good ye have sent before for your souls, ye shall find it with God; surely God seeth that which ye do. Chap. ii. Vol. i. p. 22.

They will ask thee what they shall bestow in alms; answer, the good which ye bestow, let it be given to parents and kindred, and orphans, and the poor, and the stranger. Chap. ii. Vol. i. p. 38.

O true believers, give alms of that which ye have bestowed on you, before the day cometh wherein there shall be no merchandizing, nor friendship, nor intercession. Chap. ii. Vol. i. p. 47.

'and followers; but chiefly applied them to the
'maintenance of those who served in his wars,
'and fought, as he termed it, in the way of God.
'His successors continued to do the same, until
'in process of time, other taxes and tributes be-
'ing imposed for the support of the government,
'they seem to have been weary of acting as al-
'moners to their subjects, and to have left the
'paying them to their consciences.'
Prelim. Disc. § iv. p. 147.

O true believers, make not your alms of none effect by reproaching, or mifchief, as he who layeth out what he hath to appear unto men to give alms, and believeth not in God and the laft day. The likenefs of fuch a one is as a flint covered with earth, on which a violent rain falleth, and leaveth it hard. They cannot profper in any thing which they have gained, for God directeth not the unbelieving people. Chap. ii. Vol. i. p. 50.

O true believers, beftow alms of the good things which ye have gained, and of that which we have produced for you out of the earth, and chufe not the bad thereof to give it in alms, fuch as ye would not accept yourfelves, otherwife than by connivance: and know that God is rich and worthy to be praifed.——And whatever alms ye fhall give, or whatever vow ye fhall vow, verily, God knoweth it; but the ungodly fhall have none to help them. If ye make your alms to appear, it is well; but if ye conceal them, and give them unto the poor, this will be better for you, and will atone for your sins: and God is well informed of that which ye do. The direction of them belongeth not unto thee; but God directeth whom he pleaseth. The good that ye shall give in alms, shall redound unto yourselves; and ye shall not give unless out of desire of seeing the face of God. And what good thing ye shall give in alms, it shall be repaid you, and ye shall not be treated unjustly; unto the poor who are wholly employed in fighting for the religion of God, and cannot go to and fro in the earth; whom the ignorant man thinketh rich because of their modesty: thou shalt know them by this mark, they ask not men with importunity; and what good ye shall give in alms, verily God knoweth it. They who distribute alms of their substance night and day, in private and in public, shall have their reward with their Lord; on them shall no fear come, neither shall they be grieved. Chap. ii. Vol. i. p. 51.

Alms are to be diftributed only unto the poor, and the needy, and thofe who are employed in collecting and diftributing the fame, and unto thofe whofe hearts are reconciled, and for the redemption of captives, and unto thofe who are in debt, and infolvent, and for the advantage of God's religion, and unto the traveller. This is an ordinance from God: and God is knowing and wife. Chap. ix. Vol. i. p. 251.

Your wealth and your children are only a temptation: but with God is a great reward. Wherefore fear God, as much as ye are able; and hear and obey: and give alms for the good of your fouls; for whofo is preferved from the covetoufnefs of his own foul, they shall profper. If ye lend unto God an acceptable loan, he will double the fame unto you, and will forgive you: for God is grateful and long fuffering, knowing both what is hidden, and what is divulged;

vulged; the mighty, the wife. Chap. lxiv. Vol. ii. p. 442.

AVARICE, &c.

Wo unto every flanderer, and backbiter: who heapeth up riches, and prepareth the fame for the time to come! He thinketh that his riches will render him immortal. By no means. Chap. civ. Vol. ii. p. 509.

BENEFICENCE.

Serve God, and affociate no creature with him; and fhew kindnefs unto parents, and relations, and orphans, and the poor, and your neighbour who is of kin to you, and alfo your neighbour who is a ftranger, and to your familiar companion, and the traveller, and the captives whom your right hands fhall poffefs; for God loveth not the proud or vain glorious, who are covetous, and recommend covetoufnefs unto men, and conceal that which God of his bounty hath given them; (we have prepared a fhameful punifhpunishment for the unbelievers;) and who bestow their wealth in charity to be observed of men, and believe not in God, nor in the last day; and whoever hath Satan for a companion, an evil companion hath he. Chap. iv. Vol. i. p. 101.

CALUMNY.

God loveth not the speaking ill of any one in public, unless he who is injured call for assistance; and God heareth and knoweth: whether ye publish a good action, or conceal it, or forgive evil, verily God is gracious and powerful. Chap. iv. Vol. i. p. 122.

CHARITY.

These (*i. e.* the just) fulfil their vow, and dread the day, the evil whereof will dispense itself far abroad; and give food unto the poor, and the orphan, and the bondman, for his sake, saying, we feed you for God' sake only: we desire no recompense from you

nor

nor any thanks: verily we dread from our Lord, a dismal and calamitous day. Wherefore the Lord shall deliver them from the evil of that day, and shall cast on them brightness of countenance and joy, &c. Chap. lxxvi. Vol. ii. p. 474.

—It is to free the captive; or to feed in the day of famine, the orphan who is of kin, or the poor man who lieth on the ground. Whoso doth this, and is one of those who believe, and recommend perseverance unto each other, and recommend mercy unto each other; these shall be the companions of the right hand. But they who shall disbelieve our signs, shall be the companions of the left hand: above them shall be arched fire. Chap. xc. Vol. ii. p. 498.

Verily the life to come shall be better for thee than this present life: and thy Lord shall give thee a reward wherewith thou shalt be well pleased. Did he not find thee an orphan, and hath he not taken care of thee?

thee? And did he not find thee wandering in error, and hath he not guided thee unto the truth? And did he not find thee needy, and hath he not enriched thee? Wherefore oppress not the orphan; neither repulse the beggar: but declare the goodness of thy Lord. Chap. xciii. Vol. ii. p. 500.

CIVILITY.

When ye are saluted with a salutation, salute the person with a better salutation, or at least return the same; for God taketh an account of all things. Chap. iv. Vol. i. p. 111.

O true believers, enter not any houses beside your own houses, until ye have asked leave, and have saluted the family thereof: this is better for you; peradventure ye will be admonished. And if ye shall find no person in the houses, yet do not enter them until leave be granted you: and if it be said unto you, return back; do you return back. This will be more decent for you; and God knoweth

knoweth that which ye do. It shall be no crime in you, that ye enter uninhabited houses, wherein ye may meet with a convenience. God knoweth that which ye discover, and that which ye conceal. Chap. xxiv. Vol. ii. p. 191.

CONVERSATION.

Dost thou not perceive that God knoweth whatever is in heaven and in earth? There is no private discourse among three persons, but he is the fourth of them; nor among five, but he is the sixth of them; neither among a smaller number than this, nor a larger, but he is with them, wheresoever they be: and he will declare unto them that which they have done, on the day of resurrection; for God knoweth all things.—

O true believers, when ye discourse privily together, discourse not of wickedness, and enmity, and disobedience toward the apostle; but discourse of justice and piety: and fear God before whom ye shall be assembled.

sembled. Verily the clandestine discourse of the infidels proceedeth from Satan, that he may grieve the true believers: but there shall be none to hurt them in the least, unless by the permission of God; wherefore in God let the faithful trust. Chap. lviii. Vol. ii. p. 424.

COVETOUSNESS and OPPRESSION.

Moreover man, when his Lord trieth him by prosperity, and honoureth him, and is bounteous unto him, saith, my Lord honoureth me: but when he proveth him by afflictions, and withholdeth his provisions from him; he saith, my Lord despiseth me. By no means: but ye honour not the orphan, neither do ye excite one another to feed the poor: and ye devour the inheritance of the weak, with undistinguishing greediness; and ye love riches, with much affection. By no means should ye do thus. When the earth shall be minutely ground to dust; and thy Lord shall come, and the angels rank by by rank; and hell on that day shall be brought nigh: on that day shall man call to remembrance his evil deeds; but how shall remembrance avail him? He shall say, would to God that I had heretofore done good works in my life time! On that day none shall punish with his punishment; nor shall any bind with his bonds. O thou soul which art at rest, return unto thy Lord, well pleased with thy reward, and well pleasing unto God: enter among my servants; and enter my paradise. Chap. lxxxix. Vol. ii. p. 496.

DEBTS.

Deal not unjustly with others, and ye shall not be dealt with unjustly. If there be any debtor under a difficulty of paying his debt, let his creditor wait till it be easy for him to do it; but if ye remit it as alms, it will be better for you, if ye knew it. And fear the day wherein ye shall return unto God, then shall every soul be paid what it hath gained,

gained, and they shall not be treated unjustly. O true believers, when ye bind yourselves one to the other in a debt for a certain time, write it down; and let a writer write between you according to justice, and let not the writer refuse writing according to what God hath taught him; but let him write, and let him who oweth the debt dictate, and let him fear God his Lord, and not diminish aught thereof. But if he who oweth the debt be foolish or weak, or be not able to dictate himself, let his agent dictate according to equity; and call to witness two witnesses of your neighbouring men; but if there be not two men, let there be a man and two women of those whom ye shall chuse for witnesses: if one of those women should mistake, the other of them will cause her to recollect. And the witnesses shall not refuse whensoever they shall be called. And disdain not to write it down, be it a large debt, or be it a small one, until its time of payment:

payment: this will be more juſt in the ſight of God, and more right for bearing witneſs, and more eaſy, that ye may not doubt. But if it be a preſent bargain which ye tranſact between yourſelves, it ſhall be no crime in you, if ye write it not down. And take witneſſes when ye ſell one to the other, and let no harm be done to the writer, nor to the witneſs; which if ye do, it will ſurely be injuſtice in you: and fear God, and God will inſtruct you, for God knoweth all things. And if ye be on a journey, and find no writer, let pledges be taken: but if one of you truſt the other, let him who is truſted return what he is truſted with, and fear God his Lord. And conceal not the teſtimony, for he who concealeth it, hath ſurely a wicked heart. God knoweth that which ye do. Whatever is in heaven and on earth is God's: and whether ye manifeſt that which is in your minds, or conceal it, God will call you to account for it, and will forgive whom he pleaſeth, and will puniſh whom he pleaſeth;

pleaseth; for God is almighty. Chap. ii. Vol. i. p. 52.

DISSENTIONS.

If two parties of the believers contend with one another, do ye endeavour to compose the matter between them; and if the one of them offer an insult unto the other, fight against that party which offered the insult, until they return to the judgment of God; and if they do return, make peace between them with equity: and act with justice; for God loveth those who act justly. Verily the true believers are brethren: wherefore reconcile your brethren; and fear God, that ye may obtain mercy. Chap. xlix. Vol. ii. p. 388.

DIVORCES.

The women who are divorced shall wait concerning themselves until they have their courses thrice, and it shall not be lawful for them to conceal that which God

hath

hath created in their wombs, if they believe in God and the last day; and their husbands will act more justly to bring them back at this time, if they desire a reconciliation. The women ought also to behave toward their husbands in like manner as their husbands should behave toward them, according to what is just: but the men ought to have a superiority over them. God is mighty and wise. Ye may divorce your wives twice; and then either retain them with humanity, or dismiss them with kindness. But it is not lawful for you to take away any thing of what ye have given them, unless both fear that they cannot observe the ordinances of God. And if ye fear that they cannot observe the ordinances of God, it shall be no crime in either of them on account of that for which the wife shall redeem herself. These are the ordinances of God; therefore transgress them not; for whoever transgresseth the ordinances of God, they are unjust doers. But if the husband divorce

divorce her a third time, she shall not be lawful for him again, until she marry another husband. But if he also divorce her, it shall be no crime in them, if they return to each other, if they think they can observe the ordinances of God; and these are the ordinances of God, he declareth them to people of understanding. But when ye divorce women, and they have fulfilled their prescribed time, either retain them with humanity, or dismiss them with kindness; and retain them not by violence, so that ye transgress; for he that doth this, surely injureth his own soul. And make not the signs of God a jest: but remember God's favour toward you, and that he hath sent down unto you the book of the Koran, and wisdom, admonishing you thereby; and fear God, and know that God is omniscient. But when ye have divorced your wives, and they have fulfilled their prescribed time, hinder them not from marrying their husbands, when they have agreed among themselves

selves according to what is honourable. This is given in admonition unto him among you who believeth in God, and the laſt day. This is moſt righteous for you, and moſt pure. God knoweth, but ye know not. Mothers after they are divorced ſhall give ſuck unto their children two full years, to him who deſireth the time of giving ſuck to be compleated; and the father ſhall be obliged to maintain them and cloath them in the mean time, according to that which ſhall be reaſonable. No perſon ſhall be obliged beyond his ability. A mother ſhall not be compelled to what is unreaſonable on account of her child, nor a father on account of his child. And the heir of the father ſhall be obliged to do in like manner. But if they chuſe to wean the child before the end of two years, by common conſent, and on mutual conſideration, it ſhall be no crime in them. And if ye have a mind to provide a nurſe for your children, it ſhall be no crime in you, in caſe ye fully pay what ye

offer her, according to that which is juft. And fear God, and know that God feeth whatfoever ye do. Such of you as die and leave wives, their wives muft wait concerning themfelves four months and ten days, and when they fhall have fulfilled their term, it fhall be no crime in you for that which they fhall do with themfelves, according to what is reafonable. God well knoweth that which ye do: and it fhall be no crime in you, whether ye make public overtures of marriage unto fuch women, within the faid four months and ten days, or whether ye conceal fuch your defigns in your minds. God knoweth that ye will remember them. But make no promife unto them privately, unlefs ye fpeak honourable words, and refolve not on the knot of marriage, until the prefcribed time be accomplifhed; and know that God knoweth that which is in your minds, therefore beware of him, and know that God is gracious and merciful. It fhall be no crime in you, if ye divorce your
wives,

wives, so long as ye have not touched them, nor settled any dowry on them. And provide for them (he who is at his ease must provide according to his circumstances, and he who is straitned according to his circumstances) necessaries according to what shall be reasonable. This is a duty incumbent on the righteous. But if ye divorce them before ye have touched them, and have already settled a dowry on them, ye shall give them half of what ye have settled, unless they release any part, or he release part in whose hand the knot of marriage is; and if ye release the whole, it will approach nearer unto piety.—And such of you as shall die and leave wives, ought to bequeath their wives a year's maintenance, without putting them out of their houses: but if they go out voluntarily, it shall be no crime in you, for that which they shall do with themselves, according to what shall be reasonable; God is mighty and wise. And unto those who are divorced, a reasonable provision is also due;

due; this is a duty incumbent on those who fear God. Chap. ii. Vol. i. p. 41.

O true believers, when ye marry women who are believers, and afterward put them away, before ye have touched them, there is no term prescribed you to fulfil toward them after their divorce: but make them a present, and dismiss them freely with an honourable dismission. Chap. xxxiii. Vol. ii. p. 280.

Those who divorce their wives, by declaring that they will for the future regard them as their mothers, and afterward would repair what they have said, shall be obliged to free a captive before they touch one another. This is what ye are warned to perform: and God is well apprized of that which ye do. And whoso findeth not a captive to redeem, shall observe a fast of two consecutive months, before they touch one another. And whoso shall not be able to fast that time, shall feed threescore poor men. Chap. viii. Vol. ii. p. 423.

O Prophet, when ye divorce women, put them away at their appointed term; and
com-

compute the term exactly: and fear God your Lord. Oblige them not to go out of their apartments, neither let them go out, until the term be expired, unless they be guilty of manifest uncleanness. These are the statutes of God: and whoever transgresseth the statutes of God, assuredly injureth his own soul. Thou knowest not whether God will bring something new to pass, which may reconcile them after this. And when they shall have fulfilled their term, either retain them with kindness, or part from them honourably: and take witnesses from among you, men of integrity, and give your testimony as in the presence of God. This admonition is given unto him who believeth in God and the last day: and whoso feareth God, unto him will he grant a happy issue out of all his afflictions; and he will bestow on him an ample provision from whence he expecteth it not: and whoso trusteth in God he will be his sufficient support; for God will surely attain his purpose.

Now hath God appointed unto every thing a determined period. As to such of your wives as shall despair having their courses, by reason of their age; if ye be in doubt thereof, let their term be three months: and let the same be the term of those who have not yet had their courses. But as to those who are pregnant, their term shall be until they be delivered of their burden. And whoso feareth God, unto him will he make his command easy. This is the command of God which he hath sent down unto you. And whoso feareth God, he will expiate his evil deeds from him, and will increase his reward. Suffer the women whom ye divorce to dwell in some part of the houses wherein ye dwell, according to the room and conveniences of the habitations which ye possess: and make them not uneasy, that ye may reduce them to straits. And if they be with child, expend on them what shall be needful, until they be delivered of their burden. And if they suckle their children

dren for you, give them their hire, and consult among yourselves, according to what shall be just and reasonable. And if ye be put to a difficulty herein, and another woman shall suckle the child for him, let him who hath plenty expend proportionably, in the maintenance of the mother and the nurse out of his plenty: and let him whose income is scanty, expend in proportion out of that which God hath given him. God obligeth no man to more than he hath given him ability to perform: God will cause ease to succeed hardships. Chap. lxv. Vol. ii. p. 443.

REMARKS.

It would be impertinent to enlarge on the natural intentions of matrimony; of which, every man's reason, and much more his feelings, give him sufficient information: as it is capable of communicating the highest earthly felicity, so can it be perverted to the greatest extremity of misery. When the ends of entering into an indissoluble engagement, on which the domestic comfort of all the future parts of our lives, so intimately depends, are frustrated! no situation can

can be conceived more intolerable; and it is painful even to think that sufferers in these circumstances should have all their fond expectations, all their social enjoyments, all their peace of mind, ruined beyond redemption! and that the laws which ought to protect the injured, should in these circumstances betray them; and often strengthen the hands of oppression! Divorces by the Christian law are discouraged, except in cases of adultery;* but numberless causes of unhappiness occur, which render the matrimonial state unsupportable, that do not offer such a plea to justify separation: and when this union, from whatever causes, becomes grievous,—for life is a dreadful term! the apostles replied very naturally—*if the case of the man be so with his wife, it is not good to marry.*†—By the Mohammedan law divorces are allowed to take place between the same persons repeatedly: here therefore the facility of separating and coming together again, not only grants the remedy wished for, but grants it to an extream; and appears to afford too great a latitude to caprice. Perhaps the golden mean may lie between them. For, let whatsoever render it disagreeable for

---

* Matth. v. 32. xix. 9. Mark x. 11, 12. Luke xvi. 18. 1 Cor. vii. 10, 11. † Matt. xix. 10.

man and wife to live with each other, the sufferer ought to be allowed recourse to an easy remedy:—but if, after separation, they were prohibited the privilege of coming together again on any consideration;* this would cause the motives of parting, to be as carefully weighed, as those of the first connexion. For if a couple found on enquiry, that notwithstanding their discontents, they had a foundation of secret tenderness for each other, which the thoughts of parting discovered, and which started at the undoing of what could not be renewed; the union which ought to subsist, would on such a result of self examination, receive a fresh cement: while those who ought to part, would be gratified with the opportunity. Many gentle honest hearts would thus be preserved from breaking, many useful lives be prolonged, many a painstaking person rescued from beggary, and many fortunes snatched from ruin. Those who failed in one adventure, might have the opportunity of trying another with more success; while those, of which there are many, with whom nobody ought to live, would be denied the dia-

---

* Moses prohibited a reunion, if an intervening marriage had taken place. Deut. xiv. 1, &c.

bolical

bolical pleafure of tormenting others to death, or of involving them in the confequences of ruinous conduct.

This would *indeed* be a law of reafonable liberty.

ENVY.

Covet not that which God hath beftowed on fome of you preferable to others. Unto the men fhall be given a portion of what they fhall have gained; and unto the women fhall be given a portion of what they fhall have gained : therefore afk God of his bounty; for God is omnifcient. Chap. iv. Vol. i. p. 100.

FORGIVENESS.

A fair fpeech and to forgive, is better than alms followed by michief. God is rich and merciful. Chap. ii. Vol. i. p. 50.

HYPOCRISY, &c.

Moreover the hypocrites fhall be in the loweft bottom of hell fire, and thou fhalt not find any to help them thence. But they who repent

repent and amend, and adhere firmly unto God, and approve the sincerity of their religion to God, they shall be numbered with the faithful; and God will surely give the faithful a great reward. Chap. iv. Vol. i. p. 122.

What thinkest thou of him who denieth the future judgment as a falsehood? It is he who pusheth way the orphan; and stirreth not up others to feed the poor. Wo be unto those who pray, and who are negligent at their prayer; who play the hypocrites, and deny necessaries to the needy. Chap. cvii. Vol. ii. p. 513.

INFIDELS.

O true believers! take not your fathers or your brethren for friends, if they love infidelity above faith; and whosoever among you shall take them for his friends, they will be unjust doers. Say if your fathers, and your sons, and your brethren, and your wives, and your relations, and your substance which ye have

have acquired, and your merchandize, which ye apprehend may not be fold off, and your dwellings wherein ye delight, be more dear unto you than God and his apoftle, and the advancement of his religion; wait, until God fhall fend his commands: for God directeth not the ungodly people. Chap. ix. vol. i. p. 242.

When ye encounter the unbelievers, ftrike off their heads until ye have made a great flaughter among them; and bind them in bonds; and either give them a free difmiffion afterward, or exact a ranfom, until the war fhall have laid down its arms. This fhall ye do, verily if God pleafed, he could take vengeance on them without your affiftance: but he commandeth you to fight his battles, that he may prove the one of you by the other. And as to thofe who fight in defence of God's true religion, God will not fuffer their works to perifh: he will guide them, and will difpofe their heart aright; and he will lead them into paradife,

of

of which he hath told them. O true believers, if ye affift God, by fighting for his religion, he will affift you againft your enemies; and will fet your feet faft: but as for the infidels, let them perifh; and their works fhall God render vain. Chap. xlvii. vol. ii. p. 376. See RETALIATION.

INHERITANCE and LEGACIES.

Men ought to have a part of what their parents and kindred leave behind them when they die: and women ought alfo to have a part of what their parents and kindred leave, whether it be little, or whether it be much; a determinate part is due to them. And when they who are of kin are prefent at the dividing of what is left, and alfo the orphans, and the poor, diftribute unto them fome part thereof; and if the eftate be too fmall, at leaft fpeak comfortably unto them. And let thofe fear to abufe orphans, who, if they leave behind them a weak offspring, are folicitous for them: let them therefore

fear

fear God, and speak that which is convenient. Surely they who devour the possessions of orphans unjustly, shall swallow down nothing but fire into their bellies, and shall broil in raging flames. God hath thus commanded you concerning your children. A male shall have as much as the share of two females: but if they be females only, and above two in number, they shall have two third parts of what the deceased shall leave; and if there be but one, she shall have the half. And the parents of the deceased shall have each of them a sixth part of what he shall leave, if he have a child; but if he have no child, and his parents be his heirs, then his mother shall have the third part. And if he have brethren, his mother shall have a sixth part, after the legacies which he shall bequeath, and his debts be paid. Ye know not whether your parents or your children be of greater use unto you. This is an ordinance from God, and God is knowing and wise. Moreover, ye may claim half

of

of what your wives shall leave, if they have no issue; but if they have issue, then ye shall have the fourth part of what they shall leave, after the legacies which they shall bequeath, and the debts be paid. They also shall have the fourth part of what ye shall leave, in case ye have no issue; but if ye have issue, then they shall have the eighth part of what ye shall leave, after the legacies which ye shall bequeath, and your debts be paid. And if a man or woman's substance be inherited by a distant relation, and he or she have a brother or sister; each of them two shall have a sixth part of the estate. But if there be more than this number, they shall be equal sharers in a third part, after payment of the legacies which shall be bequeathed, and the debts, without prejudice to the heirs. Chap. iv. vol. i. p. 93.

We have appointed unto every one kindred, to inherit part of what their parents and relations shall leave at their deaths. And unto those with whom your right hands have

have made an alliance, give their part of the inheritance; for God is witnefs of all things. Men fhall have the preheminence above women, becaufe of thofe advantages wherein God hath caufed the one of them to excel the other, and for that which they expend of their fubftance in maintaining their wives. Chap. iv. vol. i. p. 101.

If a man die without iffue, and have a fifter, fhe fhall have the half of what he fhall leave; and he fhall be heir to her, in cafe fhe have no iffue. But, if there be two fifters, they fhall have between them, two third parts of what he fhall leave; and if there be feveral, both brothers and fifters, a male fhall have as much as the portion of two females. God declareth unto you thefe precepts, left you err; and God knoweth all things. Chap. iv. vol. i. p. 127.

REMARKS.

The Turkifh empire was founded on conqueft; the prince is the fountain of property, and may be confidered as a perfect defpot: yet, under this defpotifm, according to the law of Mohammed, by which the private concerns of the fubject are to be regulated; fucceffion is more equitably fettled, than it is by the feudal fyftems which have obtained in other parts of Europe. It is true that commerce and the arts have in the latter, given commercial and monied property, fuch a counterbalance to that of land, that landed property has gradually loft much of its tyrannic influence; and the forms of government firft founded on thefe military tenures, have mellowed down to more equitable fyftems, in proportion to their attention to thefe objects. But, if the Ottomans at any time, feized by the contagion of literature, fhould come to underftand the native rights of mankind better, and by commerce to poffefs an influence which may enable them to avail themfelves of their knowlege againft their haughty Sultans; this fundamental advantage, of a partition of inheritance, would, fo far as it obtained in ufe, give them great advantages over ftates where landed property continues fubject to its antient limitations, while their fovereigns have loft that afcendancy and military ftrength it formerly procured them. If we confider the extenfive fize of this vaft empire, and conceive it freed from the oppreffive government under which its inhabitants groan, and become full of people, springing from the allowance of polygamy; they would under such circumstances promise fairer for universal empire, than any cramped state where land is tied up, where numbers of people are continually drained off from society, and buried in religious celibacy; and where preposterous restrictions obstruct the entrance into matrimony, to the eventual check of propagation: or if an extension of knowledge and popular vigour, should break the orientals into separate independencies, they would in all probability flourish in arts, commerce, and maritime strength, while Europe, in either case, declining, may see all these blessings by a reflux retire back to those climes from whence they first dawned on mankind.

JUSTICE.

We have sent down unto thee the book of the Koran with truth, that thou mayest judge between men through that wisdom which God sheweth thee therein; and be not an advocate for the fraudulent, but ask pardon of God for thy wrong intention, since God is indulgent and merciful. Dispute not for those

those who deceive one another, for God loveth not him who is a deceiver or unjust. Such conceal themselves from men, but they conceal not themselves from God; for he is with them when they imagine by night a saying which pleaseth him not; and God comprehendeth what they do. Behold ye are they who have disputed for them in this present life; but who shall dispute with God for them on the day of resurrection, or who will become their patron? Yet he who doth evil, or injureth his own soul, and afterward asketh pardon of God, shall find God gracious and merciful. Chap. iv. vol. i. p. 115.

Assist one another according to justice and piety; but assist not one another in injustice and malice: therefore fear God; for God is severe in punishing. Chap. v. vol. i. p. 128.

O true believers! observe justice when ye appear as witnesses before God, and let not hatred toward any induce you to do wrong;

wrong; but act juftly; this will approach nearer unto piety; and fear God; for God is fully acquainted with what ye do. Ch. v. vol. i. p. 131.

O my people, give full meafure, and juft weight, and diminifh not unto men ought of their matters; neither commit injuftice in the earth, acting corruptly. The refidue which fhall remain unto you as the gift of God, after ye fhall have done juftice to others, will be better for you than wealth gotten by fraud; if ye be true believers. Chap. ii. vol. ii. p. 29.

Woe be unto thofe who give fhort meafure or weight; who, when they receive by meafure from other men, take the full; but when they meafure unto them, or weigh unto them, defraud! Do not thofe think they fhall be raifed again at the great day; the day whereon mankind fhall ftand before the Lord of all creatures? By no means. Chap. lxxxiii. vol. ii. p. 486.

MARRIAGE.

And if ye fear that ye shall not act with equity toward orphans of the female sex, take in marriage of such other women as please you, two, or three, or four, and not more *. But if ye fear that ye cannot act equitably toward so many, marry one only, or the slaves which ye shall have acquired. This will be easier, that ye swerve

---

* The above limitation justifies what Sale remarks on this subject. 'Several learned men
'have fallen into the vulgar mistake, that Mo-
'hammed granted to his followers an unbounded
'plurality; some pretending that a man may
'have as many wives, and others, as many
'concubines, as he can maintain: whereas, ac-
'cording to the express words of the Koran, no
'man can have more than four, whether wives
'or concubines.——Nor can we urge as an ar-
'gument against so plain a precept, the cor-
'rupt manners of his followers, many of whom,
'especially men of quality and fortune, indulge
'themselves in criminal excesses; nor yet the
'example of the prophet himself, who had pe-
'culiar privileges in this and other points.'
Prelim. Disc. § vi. p. 176.

not from righteousness. And give women their dowry freely; but if they voluntarily remit unto you any part of it, enjoy it with satisfaction and advantage. Chap. iv. vol. i. p. 92.

O true believers, it is not lawful for you to be heirs of women against their will, nor to hinder them from marrying others, that ye may take away part of what ye have given them in dowry; unlefs they have been guilty of a manifest crime, but converse kindly with them. And if ye hate them, it may happen that ye may hate a thing wherein God hath placed much good. If ye be desirous to exchange a wife for another wife, and ye have already given one of them a talent, take not away any thing therefrom: will ye take it by slandering her, and doing her manifest injustice? And how can ye take it, since the one of you hath gone in unto the other, and they have received from you a firm covenant? Marry not women whom your fathers have had to wife, (except

(except what is already paſt) for this is uncleanneſs, and an abomination, and an evil way. Ye are forbidden to marry your mothers, and your daughters, and your ſiſters, and your aunts, both on the father's and on the mother's ſide, and your brother's daughters, and your ſiſter's daughters, and your mothers who have given you ſuck, and your foſter ſiſters, and your wives mothers, and your daughters in law, who are under your tuition, born of your wives, unto whom you have gone in, (but if ye have not gone in unto them, it ſhall be no ſin in you to marry them) and the wives of your ſons, who proceed out of your loins; and ye are alſo forbidden to take to wife two ſiſters, except what is already paſt; for God is gracious and merciful. Ye are alſo forbidden to take to wife free women who are married, except thoſe women whom your right hands ſhall poſſeſs as ſlaves. This is ordained you from God. Whatever is beſide this is allowed you; that ye may with

with your substance provide wives for yourselves, acting that which is right, and avoiding whoredom. And for the advantage which ye receive from them, give them their reward, according to what is ordained: but it shall be no crime in you to make any other agreement among yourselves, after the ordinance shall be complied with; for God is knowing and wise. Whoso among you hath not means sufficient that he may marry free women, who are believers, let him marry with such of your maid-servants whom your right hands possess, as are true believers; for God well knoweth your faith. Ye are the one from the other; therefore, marry them with the consent of their masters, and give them their dower according to justice; such as are modest, not guilty of whoredom, nor entertaining lovers. And when they are married, if they be guilty of adultery, they shall suffer half the punishment which is appointed for the free women. This is allowed unto him

among

among you, who feareth to fin by marrying free women; but if ye abstain from marrying slaves, it will be better for you; God is gracious and merciful. Ch. iv. vol. i. p. 96.

Marry those who are single among you, and such as are honest of your men-servants, and your maid-servants; if they be poor, God will enrich them of his abundance; for God is bounteous and wise. And let those who find not a match, keep themselves from fornication, until God shall enrich them of his abundance. And unto such of your slaves as desire a written instrument, allowing them to redeem themselves on paying a certain sum, write one, if ye know good in them, and give them of the riches of God, which he hath given you. And compel not your maid-servants to prostitute themselves, if they be willing to live chastely; that ye may seek the casual advantage of this present life: but whoever shall compel them thereto, verily God will be gracious and merciful unto such women

after

after their compulsion. Chap. xxiv. vol. ii. p. 193.

REMARKS.

Marriage admits of a twofold consideration; first, as it respects propagation, which is the primary intention of it, in a political view; and secondly, as it respects domestic felicity, which is the primary intention of it in individuals.

The first requires a freedom of investigation, which can no where be so properly indulged as upon paper; since it will not admit of being discussed in all companies, where the soft and tender circumstances on which the latter depends, may without offence be dwelt upon. In conversation it is rude to urge any thing which may shock the delicacy of those who may be confined to hear it; it is otherwise in writing: some things will better bear reading than hearing; and whenever a subject becomes tedious or disagreeable, the reader is instantly relieved by closing the book. This therefore is premised as a saving apology to ward off any charge of indelicacy which may happen to be brought by any too scrupulous reader, male or female, whose curiosity has led them to this page; where the difficult task is attempted of enquiring into, if possible, without offending any one, a subject which

which furnishes vulgar wit and brutal manners with their most disgustful allusions.

Plurality of women then, in few words, appears most undoubtedly conducive to increase what are justly esteemed the riches of a nation: for whatever may be thought of a man's enervating himself among a number of women, it does not necessarily follow that he must ruin his constitution because he may do it; any more than that every man who loves venison and madeira, and whose pocket will gratify him with both; must therefore die of a surfeit of the one, or keep himself in a continual state of intoxication with the other. Moderation is true luxury.

In christian countries matrimony is far from yielding that increase of people of which it might be capable: since all that time is totally lost to propagation, in which a man's *only* wife is breeding; yet women are far from being scarce. It may be pardonable to hint, that we appear to understand the nature of propagation much better, where, as individuals, we are interested to promote it, in a commercial view; without descending to what may be deemed gross illustrations.

The christian religion rather looks with an unfavourable eye on the married state than other-

otherwife *; and the apoſtle Paul pleads for celibacy † without referve. Hence many thouſands of young men and women are continually withdrawn from all the duties of fociety, and immured, facred to unprofitable rites, to lazineſs, to repentance, and hypocrify; and as if the remainder were thought too many to carry on the great work of raifing up pofterity, the utmoſt difcouragements and difficulties are caſt in nature's way to impede her progreſs.

Tantum relligio potuit fuadere, &c.

Hitherto marriage has been confidered only as it affects propagation; if we come to confider it in the fecond place, with an eye of calm reafon, as the means of domeſtic happineſs to individuals; we ſhall view it perhaps in a fomewhat different light; and be inclined to confeſs that an union with *one* woman of worth and virtue, muſt afford the moſt refined fatisfaction. But all men are not fentimental in their affections: if therefore poligamy were tolerated by law, men of moderation and reflexion, might ſtill confine themfelves within their own limits, and not be the leſs happy with fingle fair ones; while their country would profit by the leſs governed paffions of the fenfual.

---

* Matt. xix. 12. † 1 Cor. ch. vii. &c.

MODESTY.

Speak unto the true believers, that they restrain their eyes, and keep themselves from immodest actions: this will be more pure for them; for God is well acquainted with that which they do. And speak unto the believing women, that they restrain their eyes, and preserve their modesty, and discover not their ornaments, except what necessarily appeareth thereof; and let them throw their veils over their bosoms, and not shew their ornaments, unless to their husbands, or their fathers, or their husband's fathers, or their sons, or their husband's sons, or their brothers, or their brother's sons, or their sister's sons, or their women, or the captives which their right hands shall possess, or unto such men as attend them, and have no need of women, or unto children, who distinguish not the nakedness of women. And let them not make a noise with their feet, that their ornaments which they hide may thereby be discovered. And be ye all turned unto God, O true

O true believers, that ye may be happy. Chap. xxiv. vol. ii. p. 192.

O true believers, let your slaves and those among you, who shall not have attained the age of puberty, afk leave of you before they come into your prefence, three times in the day, namely, before the morning prayer, and when ye lay afide your garment at noon, and after the evening prayer. Thefe are the three times for you to be private: it shall be no crime in you or in them, if they go in to you without afking permiffion, after thefe times, while ye are in frequent attendance, the one of you on the other. Thus God declareth his figns unto you; for God is knowing and wife. And when your children attain the age of puberty, let them afk leave to come into your prefence at all times, in the fame manner as thofe who have attained that age before them, afk leave. Thus God declareth his figns unto you, for God is knowing and wife. As to fuch women as are paft child-bearing,

bearing, who hope not to marry again, because of their advanced age, it shall be no crime in them if they lay aside their outer garments, not shewing their ornaments; but if they abstain from this it will be better for them. God both heareth and knoweth. It shall be no crime in the blind, nor shall it be any crime in the lame, neither shall it be any crime in the sick, or in yourselves, that ye eat in your houses; or in the houses of your fathers, or the houses of your mothers, or in the houses of your brothers, or in the houses of your sisters, or the houses of your uncles on the father's side, or the houses of your aunts on the father's side, or the houses of your uncles on the mother's side, or the houses of your aunts on the mother's side, or in those houses the keys whereof ye have in your possession, or in the house of your friend. It shall not be any crime in you whether ye eat together or separately. Id. p. 198.

H MUR-

MURDER.

O true believers, the law of retaliation is ordained you for the slain; the free shall die for the free, and the servant for the servant, and a woman for a woman: but he whom his brother shall forgive, may be prosecuted, and obliged to make satisfaction according to what is just, and a fine shall be set on him with humanity. This is indulgence from your Lord, and mercy. And he who shall transgress after this, by killing the murderer, shall suffer a grievous punishment. And in this law of retaliation ye have life, O ye of understanding! that peradventure ye may fear. Chap. ii. vol. i. p. 31.

It is not lawful for a believer to kill a believer, unless it happen by mistake; and whoso killeth a believer by mistake, the penalty shall be the freeing a believer from slavery, and a fine to be paid to the family of the deceased, unless they remit it as alms: and if the slain person be of a people at enmity with you, and be a true believer, the penalty shall be the freeing of a believer; but if he be of a people in confederacy with you, a fine to be paid to his family, and the freeing of a believer. And he who findeth not wherewith to do this, shall fast two months confecutively, as a penance enjoined from God; and God is knowing and wife. But whoso killeth a believer defignedly, his reward shall be hell; he shall remain therein for ever; and God shall be angry with him, and shall curfe him, and shall prepare for him a great punifhment. Chap. iv. vol. i. p. 112.

REMARKS.

This method of accepting a pecuniary compromife for blood, we are told in a note on the paffage, from Chardin, is frequently practifed among the Mohammedans, especially in Perfia. A fimilar ufage obtained among our Saxon anceftors, where this kind of retaliatory revenge was allowed, as may be feen in our law books, under the name of *deadly feud*; and which alfo admitted of commutation for money. This indeed

deed is holding the life of a man very cheap, and rendering it infecure. But if our old Saxon laws and the prefent practice of the Afiatics do not fufficiently eftimate and guard the lives of the innocent, our prefent Englifh laws do not fet a proper value on the lives of the guilty. The prefent lift, and growing number, of capital offences in our ftatutes, is fhocking to humanity, efpecially when it appears that fuch fanguinary means are really difproportioned to their end, and prove ineffectual. It is hoped a few thoughts may be farther indulged on this ferious fubject.

There appear but two ends to be obtained by penal inflictions. I. The reformation of the offender. II. The deterring others from the commiffion of the like crimes.

Thefe two ends, however, ought to be feparately or jointly attended to, in proportion to the nature of the offence, and its detriment to fociety: and it is alfo to be confidered, whether the offence is only the refult of fome temporary paffion, of which the fubject, with proper treatment, may be cured: Or,

Whether its atrocioufnefs evinces a depravity of heart, which the fafety of mankind claims a fecurity againft; where reformation is improbable, or too precarious to be trufted.

Accord-

According as these considerations agree together, they will determine whether the first intention of punishment, respecting the reclaiming the criminal, ought to be attended to; or whether the second should be the sole object of proceeding.

From this view of the matter, who can avoid pitying poor young fellows, whose existence is cut off in the prime and vigour of life, for the paltry theft of a handkerchief, or of a watch; or for writing a few words on a slip of paper, with a fraudulent intention?

Let not the honest reader start at the light mention of these offences; the heinousness of infesting the public roads, and disturbing the intercourse of mankind, cannot be palliated; the obligation of preserving sacred that mutual confidence, without which commerce cannot be carried on, is not to be weakened: but we should not at the same time overlook *the value of a man's life!* not merely to himself, but chiefly to his country? A consideration, which nothing but the frequent lavishment of lives can occasion us to esteem so lightly: a lavishment, which subsists after it has, in great measure, destroyed its effect.

But surely, means of intimidation cannot be wanting, even though every gallows were chopped down, and though we discontinued the absurd custom of peopling our own colonies with the outcasts of their mother country. The states bordering on the Mediterranean have their gallies; and have not we roads to make and mend? Have not we other public works to execute? Have not we tin-mines, lead-mines, iron-mines, coal-pits, in plenty? Have not we manufactures to carry on, which are injurious to the human system? There are plenty of methods to employ those, who, having offended against the laws of their country, have lost all claims to the benefit of them.

According to the nature of their offences, malefactors might be made to spend their time in making some sort of reparation for the damage they have formerly done to their country. The slave for life might be converted to a useful servant of society, instead of being unprofitably hanged and forgotten; and might live a continual memorandum of his crime and punishment. The slave for time, when his slavery expired, would, by a habit of labour, and, by having been a witness of the punishment of others, take care how he endangered his liberty again. By being hard worked, and abstemiously kept, their passions would abate, they would have leisure and inclination for reflection;

flection; and, by having due care taken of their morals, would become prudent men. How different this plan from that of transporting and maintaining colonies of villains! from that of making unthinking miscreants sing psalms with halters round their necks, through the stupefaction of fear, brought on by the precipitate teazings of an Ordinary, hackneyed in the profession; and then blotting them out from the book of life.

These loose hints are left with those who may chance to think them worthy consideration; with a wish that the time may come, when ceasing to gratify the profligate and desperate, by hanging them out of the way, they may be made to *tremble* at the apprehensions of a life of *labour*.

OATHS.

Make not God the object of your oaths, that ye will deal justly, and be devout, and make peace among men; for God is he who heareth and knoweth. God will not punish you for an inconsiderate word in your oaths; but he will punish you for that which your hearts have assented unto. Chap. ii. vol. i. p. 40.

God will not punish you for an inconsiderate word in your oaths; but he will punish you for what ye solemnly swear with deliberation. And the expiation of such an inconsiderate oath shall be the feeding of ten poor men with such moderate food as ye feed your own families withal; or to cloath them; or to free the neck of a true believer from captivity: but he who shall not find wherewith to perform one of these three things, shall fast three days. This is the expiation of your oaths when ye swear inadvertently. Therefore keep your oaths. Chap. v. vol. i. p. 148.

Whoever shall violate his oath, will violate the same to the hurt only of his own soul; but whoever shall perform that which he hath covenanted with God, he will surely give him a great reward. Ch. xlviii. vol. ii. p. 382.

ORPHANS.

They will also ask ye concerning orphans: answer, to deal righteously with them is best;
and

and if ye intermeddle with the management of what belongs to them, do them no wrong; they are your brethren: God knoweth the corrupt dealer from the righteous; and if God please, he will surely distress you, for God is mighty and wise. Chap. ii. vol. i. p. 39.

And give the orphans, when they come to age, their substance; and render them not in exchange bad for good: and devour not their substance, by adding it to your own substance; for this is a great sin.——

And give not unto those who are weak of understanding the substance which God hath appointed you to preserve for them; but maintain them thereout, and cloath them, and speak kindly unto them. And examine the orphans until they attain the age of marriage: but if ye perceive they are able to manage their affairs well, deliver their substance unto them; and waste it not extravagantly, or hastily, because they grow up. Let him who is rich abstain entirely from the orphans estates; and let him
who

who is poor take thereof, according to what shall be reasonable. And when ye deliver their substance unto them, call witnesses thereof in their presence: God taketh sufficient account of your actions. Chap. iv. vol. i. p. 92.

PARENTS.

Thy Lord hath commanded that ye worship none beside him; and that ye shew kindness unto your parents, whether the one of them or both of them attain to old age with thee. Wherefore say not unto them, Fye on you! neither reproach them; but speak respectfully unto them; and submit to behave humbly toward them, out of tender affection, and say, O Lord have mercy on them both, as they nursed me when I was little. Chap. xvii. vol. ii. p. 99.

We have commanded man concerning his parents, (his mother carrieth him in her womb with weakness and faintness, and he is weaned in two years) saying, Be grateful unto me and to thy parents. Unto me shall

shall all come to be judged. But if thy parents endeavour to prevail on thee to associate with me that concerning which thou hast no knowlege, obey them not: bear them company in this world in what shall be reasonable; but follow the way of him who sincerely turneth unto me. Chap. xxxi. vol. ii. p. 263.

PATIENCE.

O true believers, be patient, and strive to excel in patience, and be constant minded, and fear God, that ye may be happy. Chap. iii. vol. i. p. 91.

PRIDE.

Distort not thy face out of contempt to men, neither walk in the earth with insolence; for God loveth no arrogant vain glorious person. And be moderate in thy pace; and lower thy voice; for the most ungrateful of all voices surely is the voice of asses. Chap. xxxi. vol. ii. p. 264.

RETALIATION.

Fight for the Religion of God, against those who fight against you, but transgress not by attacking them first, for God loveth not the transgressors. And kill them wherever ye find them, and turn them out of that whereof they have dispossessed you; for temptation to Idolatry is more grievous than slaughter: yet fight not against them in the holy temple, until they attack you therein; but if they attack you, slay them there. This shall be the reward of the infidels. But if they desist, God is gracious and merciful. Fight therefore against them, until there be no temptation to Idolatry, and the religion be God's: but if they desist, then let there be no hostility, except against the ungodly. A sacred month for a sacred month, and the holy limits of Mecca, if they attack you therein, do ye also attack them therein in retaliation; and whoever transgresseth against you by so doing, do ye transgress against him in like manner as he hath

hath tranfgreffed againſt you, and fear God, and know that God is with thofe that fear him. Contribute out of your fubſtance toward the defence of the religion of God, and throw not yourfelves with your own hands, into perdition; and do good, for God loveth thofe who do good. Chap. ii. Vol. i. p. 34.

Fear not men but fear me; neither fell my figns for a fmall price. And whofo judgeth not according to what God hath revealed, they are infidels. We have therein commanded them, that they fhould give life for life, and eye for eye, and nofe for nofe, and ear for ear, and tooth for tooth; and that wounds fhould alfo be punifhed by retaliation: but whoever fhould remit it as alms, it fhould be acepted as an atonement from him. And whofo judgeth not according to what God hath revealed, they are unjuft. Chap. v. Vol. i. p. 139.

Whoever fhall take a vengeance equal to the injury which hath been done him, and

fhall

shall afterward be unjustly treated; verily God will assist him: for God is merciful, and ready to forgive. Chap. xxii. Vol. ii. p. 175.

REMARKS.

The Hebrews under the profession of executing the vengeance of God against idolaters, acted *offensively* toward the inhabitants of Canaan; and exterminated them to settle themselves in their country: and to shew the sublimity of the christian doctrine, it is usual to instance those precepts wherein forbearance, resignation, and acquiescence under all injuries and violence, are recommended.* These are two evident extreams: the Mohammedans appear to fill up the mean between them; as being allowed to resist violence, but to act only *defensively*: nevertheless, though admitting the *lex talionis*, yet correcting the licence by representing forgiveness, or remitting of resentment, as the most commendable; and which they incline the most to, may be seen in the Introduction. A small share of common sense will enable a person to compare the conduct hinted at in the first instance, with our *pre-*

---

* Matth. v. 38, &c. Luke vi, 27, &c. 1 Cor. vi. 7.

sent ideas of juftice and morality: however, the Jews muft be allowed to be at leaft confiftent with *their* own principles, and to be in fome meafure out of the queftion; as worfhipping a God of VENGEANCE,* whom they by a metaphor ftiled A CONSUMING FIRE .‡ If it be true that the chriftians and muffulmen derived their ideas of God from the Jews, it muft at the fame time be admitted that his attributes have been greatly altered under thofe two difpenfations. Returning then to our firft fubject, it may be obferved that the mohammedan precepts feem rather better adapted in this inftance, to the nature and fituation of mankind, than the chriftian; the former being exprefsly *permitted* to have recourfe to what chriftians are *obliged* to practice, in violation of the meeknefs recommended in the gofpel: experience proving that no community can fubfift upon ftrict chriftian principles. If then fuch exhortations are found to contain impoffible precepts, and are to be received *cum mica falis*; it does not appear how any encomium can be truly founded on the literal reading of them.

---

* Deutr. xxxii. 35. 41, &c.
‡ Deutr. iv. 24. ix. 3. &c.

Bifhop

Bishop Warburton in his Alliance between Church and State, p. 304. giving his sentiments on Toleration, declares it as his opinion, that " the " Quaker who believes even defensive war to be " unchristian, should be excluded, in States upon " the continent, the common liberty of resid- " ing in frontier places." Such an one is nevertheless truly orthodox in his belief: nor is this the only instance where some persons enjoy the privilege of acting up to their principles, at the expence of the violation of them in others.

RIGHTEOUSNESS, defined.

It is not righteousness that ye turn your faces in prayer toward the east and the west, but righteousness is of him who believeth in God and the last day, and the angels, and the Scriptures, and the prophets; who giveth money for God's sake unto his kindred, and unto orphans, and the needy, and the stranger, and those who ask, and for redemption of captives; who is constant at prayer, and giveth alms; and of those who perform their covenant, when they have covenanted and who behave themselves patiently in adversity

versity and hardships, and in time of violence: these are they who are true, and these are they who fear God. Chap. ii. Vol. i. p. 31.

SCOFFING, SLANDER, ABUSE, &c.

O true believers, let not men laugh other men to scorn; who peradventure may be better than themselves: neither let women laugh other women to scorn; who may possibly be better than themselves. Neither defame one another; nor call one another by opprobrious appellations. An ill name it is to be charged with wickedness, after having embraced the faith: and whoso repenteth not, they will be the unjust doers. O true believers, carefully avoid entertaining a suspicion of another: for some suspicions are a crime. Enquire not too curiously into other men's failings: neither let the one of you speak ill of another in his absence. Would any of you desire to eat the flesh of his dead brother. Surely ye would abhor it.

it. And fear God: for God is easy to be reconciled, and merciful. Chap. xlix. Vol. ii. p. 389.

TESTAMENTS.

It is ordained you, when any of you is at the point of death, if he leave any goods, that he bequeath a legacy to his parents, and kindred, according to what shall be reasonable. This is a duty incumbent on those who fear God. But he who shall change the legacy, after he hath heard it bequeathed by the dying person, surely the sin thereof shall be on those who change it, for God is he who heareth and knoweth. Howbeit, he who apprehendeth from the testator any mistake or injustice, and shall compose the matter between them; that shall be no crime in him, for God is gracious and merciful. Chap. ii. Vol. i. p. 32.

O true believers! let witnesses be taken between you, when death approaches any of you, at the time of making the testament;

let

let there be two witnesses, just men from among you; or two others of a different tribe or faith from yourselves, if ye be journeying in the earth, and the accident of death befal you. Ye shall shut them both up after the afternoon prayer, and they shall swear by God, if ye doubt them, and they shall say, we will not sell our evidence for a bribe, although the person concerned be one who is related to us; neither will we conceal the testimony of God, for then should we certainly be of the number of the wicked. But if it appear that both have been guilty of iniquity, two others shall stand up in their place, of those who have convicted them of falshood, the two nearest in blood, and they shall swear by God, saying, Verily our testimony is more true than the testimony of these two, neither have we prevaricated; for then should we become of the number of the unjust. This will be easier, that men may give testimony according to the plain intention thereof; or fear left a different oath be given, after their oath. Therefore fear God, and hearken; for God directeth not the unjuſt people. Chap. v. Vol. i. p. 152.

THEFT.

If a man or woman ſteal, cut off their hands, in retribution for that which they have committed; this is an exemplary puniſhment appointed by God; and God is mighty and wiſe. But whoever ſhall repent after his iniquity, and amend, verily God will be turned unto him; for God is inclined to forgive, and merciful. Chap. v. Vol. i. p. 137.

TOLERATION.

Let there be no violence in Religion. Chap. ii. Vol. i. p. 48.

USURY.

They who devour uſury, ſhall not ariſe from the dead, but as he ariſeth whom Satan hath infected by a touch: this ſhall happen to them becauſe they ſay, truely ſelling

is

is but as usury: and yet God hath permitted selling, and forbidden usury. He therefore, who when there cometh unto him an admonition from his Lord, abstaineth from usury for the future, shall have what is past forgiven him, and his affair belongeth to God. But whoever returneth to usury, they shall be the companions of hell fire; they shall continue therein for ever. God shall take his blessing from usury, and shall increase alms: for God loveth no infidel, or ungodly person. But they who believe, and do that which is right, and observe the stated times of prayer, and pay their legal alms, they shall have their reward with their Lord: there shall come no fear on them, neither shall they be grieved. O true believers, fear God, and remit that which remaineth of usury, if ye really believe; but if ye do not, hearken unto war, which is declared against you from God and his apostle: yet if ye repent, ye shall have the capital of your money. Chap. ii. Vol. i. p. 52.

WHOREDOM and ADULTERY.
REMARK.

A following extract referring to a punishment of adultery, though no such punishment is specified in the Koran; this deficiency will be supplied by attending to a passage in Sale's Preliminary Discourse, which is as follows.

'There being some passages in the Koran
'which are contradictory, the mohammedan doc-
'tors obviate any difficulty from thence, by the
'doctrine of *abrogation*: for they say, that God
'in the Koran commanded several things which
'were for good reasons afterwards revoked and
'abrogated.*

'Passages abrogated are distinguished into
'three kinds: the first, where the letter and
'sense are both abrogated; the second, where
'the letter only is abrogated, but the sense re-
'mains; and the third, where the sense is abro-
'gated, though the letter remains.——

'Of the second kind is a verse called the
'verse of stoning, which according to the tra-
'dition of Omar afterward Khalif, was extant
'while

---

* A very convenient doctrine this, and if adopted by our doctors, would remove many occasions of schism among us.

'while Mohammed was living, though it be
'not now to be found. The words are thefe.
"Abhor not your parents, for this would be
"ingratitude in you. If a man and woman
"of reputation commit adultery, ye fhall ftone
"them both; it is a punifhment ordained by
"God; for God is mighty and wife."

Prelim. Difc. § iii. p. 87.

If any of your women be guilty of whoredom, produce four witneffes from among you againft them, and if they bear witnefs againft them, imprifon them in feparate apartments until death releafe them, or God affordeth them a way to efcape. Chap. iv. Vol. i. p. 95.

The whore and the whoremonger, fhall ye fcourge with an hundred ftripes. And let not compaffion toward them prevent you from executing the judgment of God; if ye believe in God and the laft day: and let fome of the true believers be witneffes of their punifhment. The whoremonger fhall not marry any other than a harlot or an
idola-

idolatress: and a harlot shall no man take in marriage, except a whoremonger or an idolater. And this kind of marriage is forbidden the true believers. But as to those who accuse women of reputation of whoredom, and produce not four witnesses of the fact, scourge them with fourscore stripes, and receive not their testimony for ever; for such are infamous prevaricators: excepting those who shall afterward repent, and amend: for unto such will God be gracious and merciful. They who shall accuse their wives of adultery, and shall have no witnesses thereof beside themselves; the testimony which shall be required of one of them shall be, that he swear four times by God, that he speaketh the truth: and the fifth time that he imprecate the curse of God on him, if he be a liar. And it shall avert the punishment from the wife, if she swear four times by God that he is a liar; and if the fifth time she imprecate the wrath of

God

God on her, if he speaketh the truth.* Chap. xxiv. Vol. ii. p. 188.

WOMEN.

O men, fear your Lord, who hath created you out of one man and out of him created his wife, and from them two hath multiplied many men and women: and fear God by whom ye beseech one another; and respect women who have borne you, for God is watching over you. Chap. iv. Vol. i. p. 92.

The honest women are obedient, careful in the absence of their husbands, for that God preserveth them, by committing them to the care and protection of the men. But

---

* 'In case both swear, the man's oath discharges him from the imputation and penalty of slander; and the woman's oath frees her from the imputation and penalty of adultery: but though the woman do swear to her innocence, yet the marriage is actually void, or ought to be declared void by the judge; because it is not fit they should continue together after they have come to these extremities. *Jallalo 'ddin.*'

those whose perverseness ye shall be apprehensive of, rebuke; and remove them into separate apartments and chastise them. But if they shall be obedient unto you, seek not an occasion of quarrel against them; for God is high and great. And if ye fear a breach between the husband and wife, send a judge out of his family, and a judge out of her family: if they shall desire a reconciliation, God will cause them to agree; for God is knowing and wise. Chap. iv. Vol. i. p. 101.

If a woman fear ill usage or aversion from her husband, it shall be no crime in them if they agree the matter amicably between themselves; for a reconciliation is better than a separation. Mens souls are naturally inclined to covetousness: but if ye be kind toward women, and fear to wrong them, God is well acquainted with what ye do. Ye can by no means carry yourselves equally between women in all respects, although

though ye study to do it; therefore turn not from a wife with all manner of aversion, nor leave her like one in suspense: if ye agree and fear to abuse your wives, God is gracious and merciful; but if they separate, God will satisfy them both of his abundance; for God is extensive and wise, and unto God belongeth whatsoever is in heaven and on earth. Chap. iv. Vol. i. p. 119.

O true believers, when believing women come unto you as refugees, try them: God well knoweth their faith. And if ye know them to be true believers, send them not back to the infidels: they are not lawful for the unbelievers to have in marriage, neither are the unbelievers lawful for them. But give their unbelieving husbands what they shall have expended for their dowers. Nor shall it be any crime in you if ye marry them, provided ye give them their dowries. And retain not the patronage of the unbelieving women: but demand back that which ye have expended for the dowry of such of
your

your wives as go over to the unbelievers; and let them demand back that which they have expended for the dowry of thofe who come over to you. This is the judgment of God which he eftablifheth among you: and God is knowing and wife. If any of your wives efcape from you to the unbelievers, and ye have your turn by the coming over of any of the unbelievers wives to you; give to thofe believers whofe wives fhall have gone away, out of the dowries of the latter, fo much as they fhall have expended for the dowries of the former: and fear God in whom ye believe. O prophet, when believing women come unto thee and plight their faith unto thee, that they will not affociate any thing with God, nor fteal, nor commit fornication, nor kill their children, nor come with a calumny which they have forged between their hands and their feet, nor be difobedient to thee in that which fhall be reafonable: then do thou plight thy faith unto them, and afk pardon for them

of

of God: for God is inclined to forgive, and is merciful: O true believers enter not into friendship with a people against whom God is incensed: they despair of the life to come, as the infidels despair of the resurrection of those who dwell in the graves. Chap. lx. Vol. ii. p. 433.

GENERAL PRECEPTS.

They will ask thee concerning wine and lots: answer, in both there is great sin, and also some things of use unto men: but their sinfulness is greater than their use. They will ask thee also what they shall bestow in alms: answer, what ye have to spare. Thus God sheweth his signs unto you, that peradventure ye might seriously think of this present world, and of the next. Chap. ii. Vol. i. p. 39.

O true believers, devour not usury, doubling it twofold; but fear God, that ye may prosper: and fear the fire which is prepared for the unbelievers; and obey God and his apostle, apoftle, that ye may obtain mercy. And run with emulation to obtain remiffion from your Lord, and paradice, whofe breadth equalleth the heavens and the earth, which is prepared for the godly; who give alms in profperity and adverfity; who bridle their anger, and forgive men: for God loveth the beneficent. And who after they have committed a crime, or dealt unjuftly with their own fouls, remember God, and afk pardon for their fins, (for who forgiveth fins except God?) and perfevere not in what they have done knowingly: their reward fhall be pardon from their Lord, and gardens wherein rivers flow, they fhall remain therein for ever: and how excellent is the reward of thofe who labour! There have already been before you examples of punifhment of infidels, therefore go through the earth and behold what hath been the end of thofe who accufe God's apoftles of impofture. Chap. iii. Vol. i. p. 79.

Say,

Say, come; I will rehearse that which your Lord hath forbidden you; that is to say, that ye be not guilty of idolatry, and that ye shew kindness to your parents, and that ye murder not your children for fear left ye be reduced to poverty: we will provide for you and them; and draw not near unto heinous crimes, neither openly, nor in secret; and slay not the soul which God hath forbidden you to slay, unless for a just cause. This hath he enjoined you that ye may understand. And meddle not with the substance of the orphan, otherwise than for the improving thereof, until he attain his age of strength; and use a full measure, and a just balance. We will not impose a task on any soul, beyond its ability. And when ye pronounce judgment observe justice, although it be for or against one who is near of kin; and fulfil the covenant of God. Chap. v. Vol. i. p. 183.

Give unto him who is of kin to you, his due, and also unto the poor, and the traveller.

veller. And waste not thy substance profusely: for the profuse are brethren of the devils: and the devil was ungrateful unto his Lord. But if thou turn from them, in expectation of the mercy which thou hopest from thy Lord; at least speak kindly unto them. And let not thy hand be tied up to thy neck; neither open it with an unbounded expansion, lest thou become worthy of reprehension, and be reduced to poverty. Verily thy Lord will enlarge the store of whom he pleaseth, and will be sparing unto whom he pleaseth; for he knoweth and regardeth his servants. Kill not your children for fear of being brought to want; we will provide for them and for you: verily the killing them is a great sin. Draw not near unto fornication; for it is wickedness, and an evil way. Neither slay the soul which God hath forbidden you to slay, unless for a just cause; and whosoever shall be slain unjustly, we have given his heir power to demand satisfaction; but let them not exceed

the

the bounds of moderation, in putting to death the murderer in too cruel a manner, or by revenging his friends blood on any other than the person who killed him; since he is assisted by this law. And meddle not with the substance of the orphan, unless it be to improve it, until he attain his age of strength: and perform your covenant, for the performance of your covenant shall be enquired into hereafter. And give full measure when you measure ought; and weigh with a just balance. This will be better and more easy for determining every man's due. And follow not that whereof thou hast no knowledge; for the hearing, and the sight, and the heart, every of these shall be examined at the last day. Walk not proudly in the land, for thou canst not cleave the earth, neither shalt thou equal the mountains in stature. All this is evil and abominable in the sight of thy Lord. These precepts are a part of the wisdom which thy Lord hath

hath revealed unto thee. Ch. xvii. Vol. ii, p. 99.

Now are the true believers happy; who humble themselves in their prayer, and who eschew all vain discourse, and who are doers of alms deeds; and who keep themselves from carnal knowlege of any women except their wives, or the captives which their right hands possess, (for as to them they shall be blameless: but whoever coveteth any woman beyond these, they are transgressors) and who acquit themselves faithfully of their trust, and justly perform their covenant; and who observe their appointed times of prayer. These shall be the heirs who shall inherit paradise, they shall continue therein for ever. Chap. xxiii. vol. ii. p. 178.

Give unto him who is of kin to thee his reasonable due; and also to the poor, and the stranger: this is better for those who seek the face of God; and they shall prosper. Whatever ye shall give in usury, to be an increase of men's substance, shall not be in-

creased

created by the blessing of God; but whatever ye shall give in alms for God's sake, they shall receive a twofold reward. Ch. xxx. vol. ii. p. 258.

Whatever things are given you, they are the provision of this present life: but the reward which is with God is better, and more durable, for those who believe and put their trust in their Lord, and who avoid heinous and filthy crimes, and when they are angry, forgive; and who hearken unto their Lord, and are constant at prayer, and whose affairs are directed by consultation among themselves, and who give alms out of what we have bestowed on them; and who, when an injury is done them, avenge themselves, (and the retaliation of evil ought to be an evil proportionate thereto:) but he who forgiveth, and is reconciled unto his enemy, shall receive his reward from God; for he loveth not the unjust doers. And whoso shall avenge himself after he hath been injured; as to these, it is not lawful to punish them for it: but it is only lawful to punish those who wrong men, and act infolently in the earth against justice; these shall suffer a grievous punishment. And whoso beareth injuries patiently, and forgiveth, verily this is a necessary work: Chap. xlii. vol. ii. p. 354.

Verily man is created extremely impatient: when evil toucheth him, he is full of complaint; but when good befalleth him, he becometh niggardly: except those who are devoutly given, and who persevere in their prayers; and those of whose substance a due and certain portion is ready to be given unto him who asketh, and him who is forbidden by shame to ask: and those who sincerely believe the day of judgment, and who dread the punishment of their Lord: (for there is none secure from the punishment of their Lord) and who abstain from the carnal knowlege of women other than their wives, or the slaves which their right hands possess; (for as to them they shall be blameless; but whoever coveteth any woman beside these, they are transgressors) and those who faithfully keep what they are entrusted with, and their covenant; and who are upright in their testimonies, and who carefully observe the requisite rites in their prayers: these shall dwell amidst gardens highly honoured. Chap. lxx. vol. ii. p. 459.

FINIS.

ADVERTISEMENT.

Juſt publiſhed, price One Shilling,

OBSERVATIONS on the NUMBER and MISERY of the POOR; on the heavy Rates levied for their Maintenance; and on the General Cauſes of Poverty: including ſome Curſory Hints for their radical Cure.

Humbly ſubmitted to public Conſideration.

Who firſt taught Souls enſlav'd, and Realms undone,
Th' enormous Faith of Many made for One?
POPE.

www.ingramcontent.com/pod-product-compliance
Lightning Source LLC
Chambersburg PA
CBHW020059170426
43199CB00009B/341